RAISED BED GARDENING FOR BEGINNERS

The Ultimate Guide To Maximizing Space For Your Garden And Growing Vegetales, Fruits, Herbs And Flowers

Carole Smith

Copyright © 2022 Carole Smith All rights reserved.

Book ISBN: 978-1-7781860-3-5

Audiobook ISBN: 978-1-7781860-4-2

No part of this guide may be reproduced in any form without permission in writing from the publisher except in the case of brief quotations embodied in critical chapters or reviews.

Legal & Disclaimer

The information contained in this book and its contents is not designed to replace or take the place of any form of medical or professional advice; and is not meant to replace the need for independent medical, financial, legal or other professional advice or services, as may be required. The content and information in this book have been provided for educational and entertainment purposes only.

The content and information contained in this book has been compiled from sources deemed reliable, and it is accurate to the best of the Author's knowledge, information and belief. However, the Author cannot guarantee its accuracy and validity and cannot be held liable for any errors and/or omissions. Further, changes are periodically made to this book as and when needed. Where appropriate and/or necessary, you must consult a professional (including but not limited to your doctor, attorney, financial advisor or such other professional advisor) before using any of the suggested remedies, techniques, or information in this book.

Upon using the contents and information contained in this book, you agree to hold harmless the Author from and against any damages, costs, and expenses, including any legal fees potentially resulting from the application of any of the information provided by this book. This disclaimer applies to any loss, damages or injury caused by the use and application, whether directly or indirectly, of any advice or information presented, whether for breach of contract, tort, negligence, personal injury, criminal intent, or under any other cause of action.

You agree to accept all risks of using the information presented inside this book.

You agree that by continuing to read this book, where appropriate and/or necessary, you shall consult a professional (including but not limited to your doctor, attorney, or financial advisor or such other advisor as needed) before using any of the suggested remedies, techniques, or information in this book.

TABLE OF CONTENTS

Introduction 1
Chapter 1 Vegetable Gardens With Raised Beds 5
Chapter 2 Ideas For Creating A Raised Bed Vegetable Garden 9
Chapter 3 How To Make A Vegetable Garden With Raised Beds 13
Chapter 4 The Vegetable Garden With Caissons 17
Chapter 5 Make A Vegetable Garden In A Box By Yourself 19
Chapter 6 The Filling Material 25
Chapter 7 How To Plan A Raised Bed 32
Chapter 8 Considerations On How To Build A Garden With Raised Beds 35
Chapter 9 The Phases Of The Construction Of Your Garden 44
Chapter 10 Design Of A Flower Bed 49
Chapter 11 Choosing The Place For Your Raised Bed 57
Chapter 12 Properly Fill A Raised Bed With Vegetables, Flowers, Or Herbs 61
Chapter 13 Plant The Raised Bed In The Fall 68
Chapter 14 Raised Beds 73
Chapter 15 Mulching 77
Chapter 16 Building A Heated Caisson 83
Chapter 17 Cultivation Tips 85
Chapter 18 Growing In Winter 90
Chapter 19 Building A Raised Bed On A Balcony 92
Chapter 20 6 Rules For A Garden On The Balcony 98
Chapter 21 Top 10 Easiest Vegetables To Grow On A Balcony 101

Chapter 22 Growing The Salad 110
Chapter 23 Growing Cucumber 113
Chapter 24 How To Repair The Garden On The Balcony From Smog 115
Chapter 25 Growing Parsley On The Balcony 118
Chapter 26 How To Grow Brussels Sprouts 119
Chapter 27 How To Grow Strawberries 126
Chapter 28 Filling A Cassette 128
Chapter 29 The "Lasagna" Vegetable Garden 130
Chapter 30 The Soil 134
Chapter 31 Create A Self-Sufficient Garden 139
Chapter 32 How To Grow Zucchini 143
Chapter 33 Growing Aromatic Plants At Home 146
Chapter 34 How To Grow Carrots 149
Chapter 35 Final Tips 154

INTRODUCTION

The vegetable garden has always been fundamental in domestic life. Even in antiquity. The philosopher Francis Bacon said that, "it was God who created the first garden". And Cicero, "next to a library you always need a garden and a vegetable garden".

Cultivating the vegetable garden has always been a habit that accompanies man from his origins.

In ancient times it was said that the garden is tiring because "the earth is low". But today a new way of growing vegetables is spreading: the raised garden (or in boxes). In this type of vegetable garden, the edges or flower beds are no longer strips in the ground bordered by curbs, but are made up of boxes (of wood, wood and metal, etc.) which raise the level of the soil, greatly facilitating the manual operations that the garden requires and saving your back! And the advantages of the raised garden do not end here: this is when it may be worthwhile to opt for this solution, as an alternative (in part or completely) to the traditional garden ...

Growing vegetables in raised boxes has at least 5 advantages compared to the traditional method, in addition to the main one, that is to considerably reduce the effort of working and, not negligible, to optimize the aesthetic impact (the raised vegetable garden tends to be generally much more decorative and neat).

1) THE IDEAL SOIL

We can fill our bins with any "mixture" of soil, leaves, aggregates and soil improvers we prefer - and therefore successfully grow vegetables that have special needs, without spilling material (generally quite expensive).

2) NO WASTE OF WATER

A drip irrigation system or even a water reserve system (through the "jars" system) can be set up in a tank, which makes the use of water extremely efficient, avoiding waste and greatly reducing the evaporation of the water.

3) VEGETABLES IN THE FOREGROUND

We can create caissons of the height that we consider most comfortable to work with (at the knee or even higher!) And we will be able to observe the plants more closely, immediately noticing damage or cultivation problems.

4) AWAY FROM SNAILS

The raised garden is particularly effective in growing classic salad greens. Cultivated on the ground, they are severely threatened by snails that adore their young shoots, while it is more difficult to reach them in a box.

5) GOODBYE WEEDS

Weeds that compete with our vegetables for nutrients can also grow in a bed, but unlike what happens on the ground, it is extremely easy to eradicate them.

Disadvantages of the raised garden compared to the traditional one? Two, in particular:

1) THE INITIAL COST

Making caissons is certainly more onerous than working the land as it is. However, it must be said that the caissons can be built using simple do-it-yourself tools, and can last many years, if you choose long-lasting materials (for example wood impregnated in an autoclave).

2) NO MACHINES

Raised gardens, in particular those at "table" height, do not allow the use of agricultural machinery (eg rotavator). However, it must be said that they are not even necessary, since the substrate that will be created in the caissons will be the ideal one for cultivation, soft and rich, without the need for mechanical processing.

Nothing detracts from the fact that the raised garden solution can be adopted even only in part, dedicating boxes to salads and aromatic plants and leaving the flower beds dedicated to tomatoes or climbing vegetables in the ground, which would not be comfortable to work in a box that is too high.

But, on balance, the raised vegetable garden method makes this activity accessible to all, particularly facilitating those with reduced mobility (for example older parents), and ultimately offering us the gifts of the earth with much less effort. It also allows those who have a terrace to garden with a good degree of productivity (thanks to the good amount of soil in the boxes) even without having a garden.

In the next chapters we will see step by step how to create your vegetable garden.

CHAPTER 1
VEGETABLE GARDENS WITH RAISED BEDS

Many times, both in vegetable gardens and in gardens, one of the longest and most complex operations is to differentiate the soil according to the type of plant; flowering plants but also vegetables and evergreens have different needs for each species, and being able to "support them" means always having beautiful plants and productive gardens.

The cultivation technique on raised beds has first and foremost the purpose and the right structural characteristics to allow this differentiation and to do it with absolute simplicity, giving you the opportunity to vary the soil according to the specific needs of your plants, so it will be easy to organize a bed for plants that love acidic soil, another for those that prefer basic soil, or little irrigation and so on; fertilizing also in a targeted manner and without waste.

In essence, this style of cultivation consists of raising the land intended for the specific plant (bed), compared to the surrounding land, and delimiting the various crops through the use of wooden planks, rather than bricks or tiles. But the advantages of this cultivation method are really many; for example, the fact you can avoid treading on the cultivated area when working it, or simply when doing maintenance or harvesting, because it is raised above the ground, you avoid compacting it, thus allowing a greater influx of air, which the roots need.

Another advantage is the increase in productivity obtained thanks to the fact that the plants can stay close to each other, since it is not necessary to provide passage ground, and in this way the problem of the growth of weeds is also very limited, consequently decreasing maintenance in general.

Furthermore, with this technique it is possible to cultivate even if you have a garden with unsuitable soil, since by raising it you can obtain an area with compost soil ad hoc for your plant, which in addition will have better drainage as it is raised, compared to compact soil, in which underlying water stagnations form (also harmful for the proliferation of fungal diseases and parasite attacks).

Raised beds are an essential part of efficient gardening. With raised beds there is no need to worry about the quality of the soil in your area. You create your ideal soil mix, ready to grow and free from weeds.

Raised beds also facilitate weeding, harvesting and crop maintenance. You can build beds from scratch or buy them off the shelf and choose the height that suits your needs.

A raised growth platform reduces the risk of back ache, as there is no need to bend over with the right size bed. My beds, for example, were built near waist height (I'm small, so it's not that high!), so I don't have to kneel or bend over too much. In a few years, I bet my back will thank me.

Another surprising benefit is that raised beds are beautiful. Unlike a series of rows on the floor, I don't have to worry about people complaining about my front beds. They look great. With the railings above the beds, my yard looks clean even when everything starts to die in the fall.

Benefits of gardening per square foot

The square foot gardening method has many benefits. The list would be long if you included them all, but here are my main reasons for preferring it to other types of gardening.

Spatial efficiency

Gardening per square foot significantly reduces the space required for crops compared to traditional inline gardening. I love the fact that in a single 4 × 4 foot bed I can grow a multitude of vegetables, from several tomato plants to a bunch of carrots.

Minimal weeding

Since everything is so close, gardening a square foot requires less weeding.

Conserve water

The soil mix you use is essential. The MPA method requires equal parts of peat, fertilizer and vermiculite.

CHAPTER 2
IDEAS FOR CREATING A RAISED BED VEGETABLE GARDEN

Many times both in the vegetable gardens and in gardens, it is necessary to differentiate the soil according to the different cultivated species; to simplify the work, also minimizing space and maintenance operations, cultivation on raised beds is used.

Vegetables and small fruits, and green or flowering plants, require, depending on the species, different soil, which has specific qualities and contains particular nutrients; being able to differentiate the soil in these cases means ensuring quality crops or blooms.

Only cultivation on raised beds lends itself perfectly to this operation and can also be used with excellent results in the creation of eye-catching flower beds and decorative green structures.

Furthermore, by exploiting a raised bed it is possible to avoid the growth and multiplication of weeds in a much simpler and faster way, as well as being able to cultivate invasive plants, such as blackberries and raspberries, rather than different vegetables or flowering species.

Soil drainage will also be better when growing on raised beds, and all varieties of plants will benefit greatly.

The materials with which raised beds can be made are many, and it will be possible to choose between wood in its various qualities, concrete, raw or worked stone, but also recycled materials and objects that can be used very well for the creation of truly original flower beds.

So let's see 9 ideas from which to take inspiration to create a raised bed with which to grow vegetables from the garden, rather than magnificent flowering varieties.

1.

By recycling an old pallet it is possible to create a raised bed perfect for any area of the garden or vegetable garden, it is a really simple and above all economical project.

2.

Even old furniture lends itself well to the creation of a raised bed. In this case the final result is truly magnificent and, positioned in a vegetable garden, this structure is able to transform it into an elegant and original place.

3.

With a good number of terracotta pots you can create a border, pretty and practical, which acts as a raised bed; a way to make the most of the cultivable space and to recycle old pots rather than other containers.

4.

Even using simple wooden planks, functional and decorative raised beds can be created; in this case the height of the bed is minimal and we decided to create a structure on two levels; perfect for growing flowering species and creating beautiful splashes of color in the garden.

5.

An aluminum tub has been reused as a large and modern container.

6. Discarded tires can be transformed into highly original raised beds in which vegetables can be grown

Recycling is always a great way to start engaging creative projects; old tires have been transformed into highly original raised beds in which vegetables, fruit or ornamental plants can be grown.

7.

A large raised bed completely built in brick; an elegant and functional structure ideal for the vegetable garden and for the garden.

8.

You can recycle perforated concrete blocks to make a raised bed, square or round.

9.

Wood can be used to give the garden a particular shape, ideal for growing flowering species mixed with vegetables and small shrubs; if you wish, you can also use other materials, modify the shape and create a truly original large flowerbed.

CHAPTER 3
HOW TO MAKE A VEGETABLE GARDEN WITH RAISED BEDS

The advantages of growing on raised beds are so many; first of all with this technique it will be much easier to differentiate the soil according to the needs of the plant, compared to the classic cultivation on the ground.

Another important advantage is that by deciding to grow vegetables, rather than aromatic herbs or flowering plants, using the raised beds technique it will also be possible to do it on the balcony, on the terrace or perhaps in an area of the garden that was previously unused because it lacks soil with the right characteristics.

In essence, this cultivation technique consists of raising the soil intended for the plants and delimiting the different crops through the construction of simple structures obtained by assembling wooden planks rather than bricks or stones of various kinds.

Let's see how to make a functional raised bed in a few simple steps.

What is needed

4 wooden planks 10 x 10 x 40 cm

2 wooden boards 5 x 30 x 120 cm

2 wooden boards 5 x 30 x 240 cm

24 wood screws 8.5 cm

24 wood screws 1,5 cm

6 PVC pipes diameter 20 mm and length 30

6 metal fittings for pipes

Method

1.

How to build a raised bed

We start construction by assembling a 120cm board with a square plank. It may be helpful to use a clamp to temporarily hold the pieces together before inserting the screws.

1. To prevent the wood from splitting, it is advisable to drill before fixing the screws.

2. Three screws will be enough for each board and three for each corner. Always make sure that the boards are aligned on the bottom with the square blocks

3. At this point we should turn the bed and look for the best position for the final installation; the chosen area must have at least 6 hours of sun exposure per day.

4. We should anchor the bed to the ground by making a hole of about 12-15 cm for each foot.

6. Having done this, it is necessary to check that the bed is level, so that the irrigation water can be distributed evenly in the ground, without causing stagnation.

7. Now is the time to install the PVC pipes, three for each side panel of the bed. The tubes will be fixed inside the bed using the metal hooks; these tubes have the function of support for the positioning of the net that will be added to the structure to protect our small garden from birds and from the cold.

8. At this point we will prepare a mixture of soil and compost and distribute it throughout the bed, taking care to moisten it well.

9. You can add a drip irrigation system by inserting one tube along the wide side of the bed and another 4 along the length.

10.

Now it will be possible to cultivate what we want, to create a small vegetable garden rather than a delightful flowery area.

11.

Finally, by attaching other curved pipes to the PVC pipes it will be possible to create a sort of protection using a plastic sheet, and thus transforming our raised bed into a small greenhouse.

CHAPTER 4
THE VEGETABLE GARDEN WITH CAISSONS

The vegetable garden with caissons is made where there is no land or where the soil is bad. So when you have only a concrete open space or soil full of debris of all kinds, do not despair: you just need to know how to equip yourself and even the most squalid space can turn into a vegetable garden or flower garden!

Generally the caissons are built with wooden planks, to be treated with non-toxic paints to make them more robust and less attackable by atmospheric agents.

We must not feel less fortunate in having to opt for the vegetable garden in a box, because it has all the advantages of the vegetable garden on raised beds, but in general its height is much higher (45-60 cm) and can contain a lot of selected soil.

Think what a relief for your back to be able to work at this height! Even the most thankless work, like weeding, will turn out to be a breeze. And if we wanted to, we could arrange the edge as a real bench: work and rest at the same time!

The caissons can also help us to create vegetable gardens on terraces, or flat roofs, the important thing is to have good waterproofing of the floors on which they are placed. The dimensions will change according to your needs.

Internally, the caissons will be filled as if they were huge pots, thus providing drainage material on the bottom (lapilli, pumice, etc.) and then on top, good soil and organic fertilizer.

Parking lots, courtyards, shafts, abandoned areas ... any place can be used to welcome a vegetable garden!

CHAPTER 5
MAKE A VEGETABLE GARDEN IN A BOX BY YOURSELF

WE HAVE created a vegetable garden in a box for which we did not spend a euro (almost). You can take cues and inspiration from the idea. Eventually, if you don't have much space and you want to make a balcony garden, think small by reducing the sizes.

Why a vegetable garden in a box?

We are lucky enough to live in the countryside and have a garden where we can have a vegetable garden. Unfortunately, we never did, discouraged by the fact that we do not have a well, the right equipment and not even the time to keep it clean and free of weeds. And then, as they say, "the earth is low ... and the back gets broken!"

But then with lockdown, the time available, the shopping once a week, the lines at the supermarket dressed as a diver ...

Let's make a vegetable garden in a box, that is, a vegetable garden made inside large cassettes raised from the ground. All I need is a watering can for water, a small rake to clean up any weeds and since it is a raised vegetable garden… less back pain.

I honestly hadn't been convinced. I thought that the idea of the vegetable garden in the box was just a stupid thing, so I remained convinced that a real garden on the ground would be better and that not being able to do it, we could continue to live without it.

Where to make a vegetable garden?

We need a place where the water is close and the ground is level.

From that conversation I forgot the subject, but in the meantime he was harboring the idea, he had already thought about where to do it and mentally made an action plan. He got information online on how to make a vegetable garden, watched videos, read a few expert sites.

In the meantime, he began, day after day, to "exhume" our old pigsty which, being unused, seemed to him the best place. Only it had long been abandoned and turned into a ruin.

So, we have, - I correct myself, H - removed the weeds, the ivy, and slowly everything began to take shape. Even the old terracotta floor has seen the light again!

Soil is also needed.

During the cleaning then, given the good smell of soil that was there, my husband saw fit to recover the earth that covered the place. So he took an old chicken coop net and before taking the soil away with the cart, he began to filter it all, removing leaves, small branches and various debris. With this system he recovered a large amount of soil.

How we built the seedling boxes

Having a nice large space available, we have built cassettes measuring 120 x 80 x 35cm rather than boxes. In fact, we recycled some wooden planks that we had put aside to make a fence that was never built.

So, equipped with an electric saw, we cut all the wooden stakes to size and built nine bottomless cassettes that we placed on top of old recycled wooden pallets.

To prevent the soil from coming out of the slats, we fixed rectangles of an old disused shade cloth on top of each pallet. Then on top of the cloth we put some wattle (we have it in the garden) cut to size to cover the bottom. In addition to supporting the weight of the earth, it also serves to keep the soil moist. Finally, to save the wood from humidity, we lined the interior walls with black sacks.

What to put inside the cassettes

Well, it's time to fill our bins. The method we used is that of filling in layers, like lasagna. Obviously we didn't invent this system but we studied it.

Basically, after covering the bottom with wattle, we put a layer of cut grass (grass mulch) on top and after a few days we filled the box with our recovered soil. Only after having let the soil settle for a while, did we plant our seedlings.

Finally, to fertilize the soil a little, as a last step we put a thin layer of manure on top, an organic fertilizer that we bought when buying the plants (the cost is modest).

Vegetable garden box: which plants to plant?

Which seedlings to plant in a vegetable garden depends a little on your tastes and also on the depth of the boxes. We have planted green beans, courgettes, cucumbers, spring onions, two varieties of tomatoes, two types of salad.

Basil and parsley, on the other hand, we planted them in the old pig feeders after having raised them and drilled them to drain the water.

Here, this was the phase of the construction of our vegetable garden in caissons which took place about two years ago.

From here on began the phase of care and love, of curiosity and beauty, of wonder and amazement in seeing nature that grows rapidly every day before our eyes.

I never would have thought that some boxes full of earth would have given us so much satisfaction. In fact, the plants have become giants, we picked our courgette flowers and green beans, tomatoes and cucumbers and the salad.

Raised garden and balcony garden: tips and tricks

If we have teased you and made you want to make your own DIY balcony garden, know that you can do it too, albeit with some modifications in case you have little space.

In addition to the area cultivated on the ground, I decided to expand the garden by cultivating in wooden boxes, to be arranged in the paved parts and make the most of the spaces.

Anyone can try to start a small vegetable cultivation, even on a balcony or terrace.

It will be satisfying and fun, taking care of the plants that will bear fruit and eating them fresh at the table!

To make the boxes, wooden pallets can be used, limiting costs and giving new life to the pallets.

If you are a DIY lover try this.

By cutting the pallet on the short side, at a height of 36 cm, I obtained the two sides of the caissons, which measure 120 cm, like the pallet itself.

Obviously you can decide the height but I found myself comfortable cutting in this way, to get the walls without too much dismantling.

Disassembling a pallet is not easy but with a little practice you will find the right way to dismantle it quickly without breaking boards, which will be used to assemble the other walls.

In fact, I have disassembled some of them to obtain boards, 120cm long and by dividing them in half I will be able to build the short 60cm walls.

You will need two posts to make a box complete with all the side walls and the bottom.

The box will therefore have a length of 120 cm, a width of 60 cm and a depth of 36 cm, sufficient to grow vegetables.

On the bottom I have fixed other boards that will support the weight of the earth when the box is full.

You can close it completely at the base or leave some gaps and apply a metal mesh on the bottom of the box as an additional support.

In fact, the boxes will be very capacious, about 250 liters of earth and therefore a lot of weight to support.

Finally, I lined the box internally with a sheet, the kind used to mulch the soil, because they drain the water but do not let the earth come out. Alternatively, you can use a specially perforated PVC sheet.

The wood would be better treated with water-based impregnations, because it wears out quite quickly under the action of atmospheric agents!

To fill the bins I built, I used the layered composting technique by adding organic matter and earthworms.

Making the containers is really fun, but trying to grow some plants in them is even more fun!

CHAPTER 6
THE FILLING MATERIAL

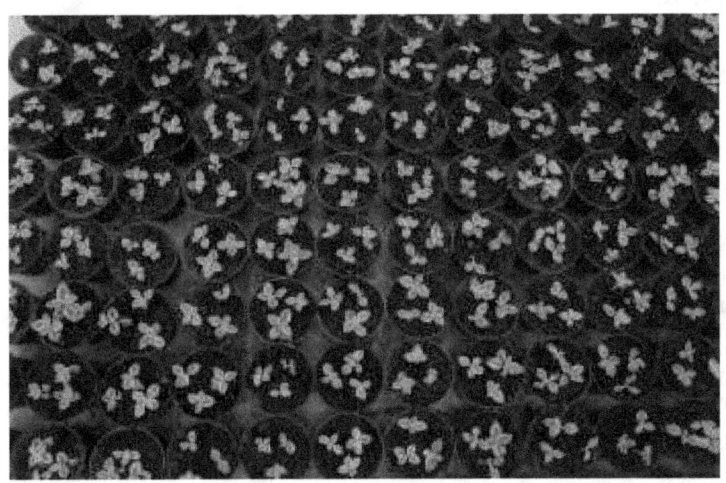

P ractical, modern and back-friendly: raised beds are trendy. If you are in possession of such a structure, you can be happy in the spring as one of the first with a crisp salad. And over the course of a long life in gardening, the high bed becomes more and more indispensable if the constant hunching causes problems and hurts your back after a long day of work. To be able to garden with a raised bed, however, it is important to fill it according to certain criteria.

Pick the optimal time

For construction and filling it is important to set the optimal time;

for example, both spring and autumn are especially suitable for applying filling. During this time, the garden typically produces hardwood or pruning wood, which can be used for backfilling.

A raised bed consists of three main layers:

Drainage

Fertilizer

Background

It does not matter what kind of raised bed is to be created: the filling material used from the bottom layer to the top layer becomes finer and finer. For example, there are branches and twigs near the bottom, in the center, compost and on the top, pot soil.

Tip: To protect the raised bed from voles, it has proved useful to lay the floor with a mouse grate.

Various raised beds for different purposes

Today, the raised bed is used for many different needs. Often hobby gardeners use them for the following purposes:

As a vegetable garden

For salad

Like a herb garden

For flowers

Depending on which applications are possible for the raised bed, the composition of the contents may vary; a classic flower bed comes with a simple layering of an air-permeable layer on the bottom, compost as the middle layer and topsoil as the final layer. Vegetables typically require additional layers. Those who want to use their raised bed as a small vegetable garden must also consider the different needs of each plant; while Mediterranean plants such as rosemary and thyme prefer dry, sandy soil, for example domestic herbs (chives or parsley) require fresh soil. If in doubt, the upper layers of earth should be divided into different areas.

Filling a classic vegetable raised bed

Each bed is individual and has certain requirements and different structural conditions. Here we show you the filling of a sample bed.

First layer: drainage layer

The first layer used to fill the raised bed is the drainage layer; this has the following properties:

A maximum thickness of 30 cm, minimum 10 cm

Water must not accumulate in the raised bed

Use stones, clay or branches

Anyone who cuts trees in his garden in the fall should carefully store the clippings to make the first layer. The branches are laid out on the raised bed floor. Then follow the thinner layers with brushwood and twigs. Alternatively, the rhizomes covered with some soil can serve as a filling of the lower layer. In addition, cardboard or cardboard boxes are suitable, but they should not be printed.

As an alternative, the first layer can be stones and shards. As with layering with plant material, the same is true here: from the bottom up, the individual components are becoming finer and finer. Thus you can find pieces of clay or larger stones on the bottom, which are then covered with clay granules or gravel.

Second layer - soil mixture

The first substrate layer is spread over the drainage layer. This layer has the following properties:

Thickness about 15 cm

Serves to support the decomposition process of the wood core

You can use garden soil or the finished substrate

Drainage is followed by a layer of semi-decomposed sod or compost covered with a layer of leaves or straw or a mixture of both. The conclusion is a mixture of sifted soil and compost.

Tip: if Mediterranean plants are to be grown, the substrate as a whole must not be too nutritious. For ornamental plants, which generally stay longer in the bed, you can always incorporate lava or expanded clay. In addition, a pH test is suitable with which the soil can be checked for acidic or alkaline properties; this is essential for the choice of vegetables.

As an alternative to the mixture of substrate from the quality soil of your own garden, many possibilities are offered by the specialized market. Again, different varieties are available for individual plant species.

Third layer: wood core

Garden waste can be optimally used for the wood core. Eg:

Thin branches, chopped

Vegetable remains (fruit, vegetables)

Remains of shrub pruning

Tip: The individual parts used to fill this layer must not exceed a total depth of approximately 40 cm!

The wooden core can be generous in its thickness; a total of 40 cm should be budgeted for this position. If the layer is thick enough, it ensures that the decomposition process provides enough nutrients and heat for the plants.

Foliage can be used to cover the wood core; the leaves should be three inches deep.

Fourth layer: central core

The central core forms the fourth layer of a raised bed. When creating the following applies:

Thickness about 15 cm

Material: manure such as horse manure or coarsely ground compost

Tip: If you want to use compost from your garden for your raised bed, you should never use it if there is meat or fish in it. In composting it should also be noted that no plastic should be in the mixture; compost should be 100% biodegradable and therefore contain only rotting food.

The wood core layer may contain in addition to the beneficial compost, organisms that are targeted. They ensure that the compost is crushed and has a faster decomposition process. For the plants, important nutrients are released in this way. If the plants have grown in the raised bed, which have an increased need for nutrients, it is also the use of a long-term fertilizer, with which the bed is enriched. Horn shavings are used for this purpose.

Fifth layer: finely sieved compost

The last layer of the raised bed is a finely sieved compost, which guarantees the nutritional supply of the plants; this way they can grow optimally. After harvesting, this layer can be refreshed if necessary before inserting new seedlings. If neither compost nor garden soil is available in your green area, you can purchase suitable substrates in the specialist market, for example:

Garden soil (for salad)

Topsoil

Mother earth (ideal for crops).

Renewal of the raised bed

The raised bed content does not remain stable throughout the year; over the months, the entire contents of the system collapse, so that the filling height is reduced by up to 20 cm. Then fresh earth must be added. Spring is best suited for this measure, as the entire plant will undergo a thorough inspection during this time.

Usually after five, but after seven years at the latest, the raised bed needs to be renewed. Then the following measures apply:

Repair construction, repair damaged areas

Completely replace content

Create layers from scratch

Background of these measures: after a few years, the nutrients contained in the filling material are completely depleted. This does not only apply to constructions that serve as a vegetable garden, but also to flower beds. Anyone who cares about his raised beds over the years, renews the filling regularly, and also does general construction, will enjoy many years of use from his beds. Hence the raised bed remains a popular highlight in the local green area. For back-friendly gardening - in old age!

CHAPTER 7
HOW TO PLAN A RAISED BED

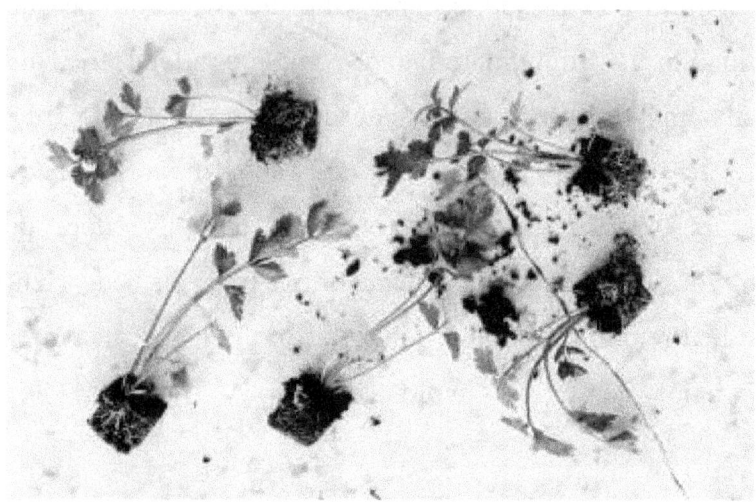

Planning a Raised Bed - These are the points to consider

Raised beds can be used and designed in many ways. They range from fruit or wine crates that have been reused, to elegant raised stone beds with ornamental plants as dividers in the garden, to clever raised table beds with herbs on the balcony or terrace. Before construction, however, comes careful planning.

What is the purpose of the raised bed?

Do you want the raised bed to be more a component of the vegetable garden and to mainly allow for practical and easy-to-access vegetable cultivation? Then a rectangular and inexpensive variant made of boards or logs is a good choice. With a little manual dexterity, you can easily build this type of raised bed yourself.

Materials suitable for building raised beds

Even faster and easier to erect are raised beds made from prefabricated plastic elements. The trade also offers composter kits made of wooden slats that can easily be converted into raised beds. If you can invest a little more, you should choose a more expensive but much more durable hardwood for the bed. Do you want your raised bed construction to be even more durable? Then raised stone beds are the first choice. However, they are more complex to build and more expensive than wooden models.

A raised bed for vegetables

Raised flower beds need a sunny, warm, spot out of the wind. Either you build them in the vegetable garden or put them near the house and terrace - then the harvesting paths are short. If you have several raised beds, you should also leave enough room on the paths for daily care. Additionally, raised beds require some effort every few years to renew the substrate.

A nice raised bed in the ornamental garden

If, on the other hand, the raised bed is not for growing vegetables but for redesigning and beautifying the garden, you should choose the materials with particular care. In addition to stone, there are also raised beds made of metal, wicker or other materials. Raised beds for ornamental plants can also be made in almost any location, for example to structure and enhance the garden.

Advice

Raised beds are usually square. However, there are also round, polygonal or curved versions. These are first-class design elements, but they are more elaborate to build than the rectangular shapes.

CHAPTER 8
CONSIDERATIONS ON HOW TO BUILD A GARDEN WITH RAISED BEDS

The first thing we must try to understand is why we should focus on this solution and if it is really essential for us.

That a raised garden is generally more orderly and aesthetically pleasing is a fact, but this has little to do with the cultivation and growth of vegetables.

But let's take a step back: what is meant by a raised garden?

These are plots, mostly dedicated to single crops, which are raised above the ground level.

Raised flowerbeds can be in masonry, wood, plastic, more or less high (i.e. deep) more or less equipped with mulch sheets, irrigation systems, etc.

STRUCTURES FOR A RAISED GARDEN

It all depends, of course, on the material used to create the flower beds and support the earth but, in general, in addition to the cost of the materials, there is a fair amount of work to be done, all the more so as the structures will be considered fixed.

It is true that to create the raised perimeter of the plots you can also reuse materials that you already have at home (wooden planks, pieces of sheet metal, stones), but it is also true that if you do not want to transform your garden into a slum, it requires a certain consistency of materials, which means having to buy them.

Why build a raised garden?

The reasons can be different, from that of an aesthetic nature, as mentioned above, to that of a practical nature, as we will see.

Now, the main reason it can be interesting to build raised beds is the poor quality of the soil.

Often we have to do with heavy soils where water stagnates or, vice versa, we have sandy and arid soils with few nutrients and where the water drains very quickly.

It becomes complicated to correct these types of soil so you can create raised boxes where you can create a soil suitable for the cultivation of most vegetables.

You can create caissons with slightly different soils depending on the type of plant that will be grown there.

All beautiful and interesting, isn't it?

Unfortunately there are also the bad points of such a project, but let's go in order.

Those who have a minimum of manual skills can certainly build a raised garden using the materials they prefer.

Generally, we start with materials that may already be available, such as old wooden planks, and then buy only the ones we need to finish the structure.

The same applies if we want to create a raised flowerbed with bricks, stones, etc.

The most important thing to do is to start with a well-defined project so as not to leave anything to chance and proceed with the purchase of only the materials necessary for the work.

Within this area we can then create several raised caissons, generally rectangular in shape, which must be separated by comfortable walkways where it is also possible to pass with a wheelbarrow, in order to make all the care and maintenance operations of the vegetable garden.

The rectangular structure is the most rational, from the point of view of space management and also the easiest to make, but it is obviously not the only one.

What height should the raised garden have?

The question to ask should be another: why do I want to build a raised garden?

If the problem is the poor quality of the soil, just create raised flower beds of about 20 cm, remember that we will then have to fill them with earth!

Obviously, in the case of particular gardens, raised caissons of 1 meter and 1 meter and a half can also be created.

This type of garden, if well built, is also accessible to wheelchair users and elderly people with limited mobility.

In the case of tall flowerbeds, it is obviously inadvisable to fill the entire structure with earth, it would really be a useless waste and, moreover, the soil would push a lot on the structure which should therefore be very solid.

In these cases it is advisable to create suspended boxes, such as those seen in greenhouses, with a depth of 20-30 cm or, alternatively, to cultivate the plants in pots above these suspended structures.

STRUCTURES FOR THE HANGING GARDEN

Remember that the inside of the caissons, especially if made of wood, must be covered with a special waterproofing fabric, in order to prevent deterioration of the wood in contact with the humidity of the ground.

In all cases, the wood must be treated, externally and internally, with an impregnating agent in order to resist atmospheric agents.

Which material to choose for the raised garden structure?

The choice of materials is very important because the raised flower beds in the garden will have to remain in their location for some time.

I wrote "for some time" and not "forever" not by chance.

Personally, I do not recommend the creation of fixed masonry structures to always leave the possibility to change, one day, or dismantle everything, without having to damage one's soul.

This does not mean that it is not possible to resort to dry masonry structures which are easy to build and dismantle.

By raised masonry gardens I therefore mean dry structures that are not bonded with cement mortar.

We can consider them as semi-permanent structures which, compared to wooden structures, in any case require a much greater commitment.

Let's now see some materials and possible structures.

Wooden planks

Wooden planks are the easiest way to make a raised bed.

The variable, in these rectangular or square structures consists of the poles to which the boards are anchored.

In one case the 4 support poles, strictly of square or triangular section, can be fixed inside the perimeter of the box and the boards will subsequently be nailed to the poles.

It is the simplest and most aesthetically pleasing solution because on the outside we only see the boards and the supporting poles do not constitute a hindrance.

A particularly suitable solution in case of little raised flower beds.

The other possibility consists in fixing 8 poles, 2 for each corner, outside the structure.

In this way the boards do not have to be nailed but will remain in position thanks to the force of the soil that will be placed inside the box.

Support posts placed outside are less visually pleasing and can be a hindrance.

The poles must always be planted firmly in the ground, remember that they must support the structure.

A third possibility, for those more experienced in carpentry work, is to fit the boards between them but even in that case we have protrusions that, personally, I do not appreciate.

In the latter case the structure is self-regulating and there is no need for poles.

Raised garden in masonry

By bricks I mean the classic solid bricks, terracotta, or perforated bricks that have a certain thickness.

In all cases, these are perfectly regular elements that can be placed on top of each other, alternating courses, to obtain dry stone walls.

In the event that the raised flower beds were particularly low, the bricks could simply be aligned vertically by burying half of their length in the ground.

If the raised bed has a certain height, the bricks must be laid in such a way that the short side remains visible and the structure as a whole is thus more solid and thicker.

Gabions, filled with stones

If you think that metal gabions are used exclusively for road containment works, you are wrong.

They can also be used to create raised gardens.

Gabions are not just those gigantic structures that we often imagine, as much slimmer structures have been put on the market, suitable for the most varied purposes.

What they have in common with their ancestors is that they are metal, with more or less large meshes, which must be filled with stones.

The advantage of these cages to create a raised vegetable garden is that, once the cage has been installed, a cost-free material such as stones can be used, perhaps by reclaiming particularly stony ground.

The containment sheet is essential to prevent it from seeping through the stones.

The final result is aesthetically valuable and the cages with the stones can eventually be disassembled and reassembled elsewhere.

Nothing forbids, obviously, creating low dry stone walls but the work would be quite burdensome and, in the absence of slightly squared stones, even difficult to build.

These are basically the three systems I recommend for creating raised flower beds.

The main advantage essentially consists in being able to improve the soil without having to work on the entire surface of the garden.

From an aesthetic point of view it is an appreciable solution, the garden is cleaner and tidier.

With raised flower beds it is more difficult for animals such as snails to attack crops, especially if we sprinkle wood ash at the base of the flower beds.

The raised garden tends to heat up faster, favoring the germination and development of plants, especially in the middle seasons.

If the flower beds are raised enough, it will greatly benefit the back and, as written above, even people with some motor disabilities can, quite easily, indulge in this hobby in the open air.

The soil, not being compacted by continuous trampling, is on average more friable and therefore suitable for the development of the root system of plants.

The plants get a little more light than the ground level and this also favors their development.

We now come to the disadvantages, which are also not lacking.

The work to be done is not easy.

The raised garden is quite expensive because to improve the quality of the soil you need to buy bags of soil, manure etc.

Raised caissons accumulate heat but also release it quickly, so providing adequate mulching of the surface is highly advisable.

The higher the flower beds, the more difficult it is to integrate drip irrigation systems.

Raised caissons, if made of untreated wood, tend to rot over time.

After filling the caissons with earth you have to wet it and wait for it to settle a little, since the loose soil has a greater volume but then tends to shrink, so wait a while before planting.

CHAPTER 9
THE PHASES OF THE CONSTRUCTION OF YOUR GARDEN

If your garden isn't as productive as hoped, or you just have a small area for gardening, creating a raised bed is the answer to all your problems.

Planning

1

View and design. Fortunately, it doesn't require any special skill or commitment - you just have to build a box of any size and shape, as long as it's open on the bottom and top sides.

2

Draw your flowerbed project, based on the space available. Now, you will know how much material you need for the actual construction.

3

Decide which materials to use. You will be able to choose from anything that can hold the earth; wood, plastic, synthetic wood, brick, rock or whatever you want or have available. Usually, the use of wood is preferable, being the simplest and most efficient method of all. This guide will focus on making flower beds using natural or synthetic wood.

4

Purchase or procure the necessary materials. The complete list is available at the bottom of the page. You will certainly need planks of the desired length, and no less than 60 cm in height. The number of planks will vary in relation to the desired shape of the flower bed.

Realization

Build the sides of your raised bed into the desired shape. If you will be using wood, you may want to try with uprights (100mm thick battens), to be placed at the corners of the bed. This technique will increase the stability of the structure, ensuring that it does not come down when the earth is laid.

2

Cut a piece of mulch (breathable or not) to the size of the bottom base of the bed - by doing so, you will significantly reduce weed growth. You could also try 7-8 layers of wet newspaper, but also old cardboard pieces from boxes. (Be sure to remove any remaining adhesive tape).

3

Place your raised bed on the mulched area. This operation could require 2 people, considering the size and weight of the structure. Make sure you choose a spot in full sun - remember, your raised bed will be nearly permanent, so you'll need to choose the best spot to place it permanently.

Usage

1

Fill it with earth. Add mature manure to the bottom and then a layer of compost soil. You can lower the costs of the work (up to 50%) by taking some soil from other areas of your property. Use 1/3 of compost, or manure.

Add and mix organic fertilizers (such as wood ash, ox blood, rock meal, etc.). Always follow the instructions for each individual product.

2

Start sowing. Some people prefer flowers, others prefer vegetables. You can choose what you want to sow.

3

Protect. To build a miniature structure for biological control of insects, you can use a greenhouse for the warm season: assemble a structure, using PVC arches along the short side of the flowerbed with an arch every 1.5 m (on the long side).

Purchase a piece of non-woven fabric, from a specialty store or on the internet, and secure it to the structure with zip ties. With this cover, you will have a wetter, warmer and more insect-proof bed.

It might sound strange, but light, heat and humidity can penetrate in just the right proportions, unlike bugs and weed seeds carried by the wind. This method will allow you to reduce watering, hand weeding and the need for pesticides.

You can use the same structure to position the nylon sheet for the colder seasons, or for more resistant protection from animals such as birds or wild boars.

Advice

Try to use 30x5 cm strips, to have 60 cm high sides.

Unleash your creativity while building. Make sure you water your flower beds frequently. Given its raised structure, it will have less water retention capacity than normal soil - placing the raised bed in a place close to the water source will greatly reduce future problems.

The ideal size should be 60 x 120cm. This is because this allows comfortable and pain-free access to the back, from all sides to the center of the flower bed (for a person of average build), without setting foot on the ground inside (and without compacting it).

Keeping the flower beds tight will help improve water retention.

Warnings

Some old pieces of treated wood - often used for external structures - may contain arsenic, a deadly and carcinogenic poison. Fortunately, these types of treatments are no longer carried out, but nonetheless there may be traces of them in ancient pieces. Arsenic is released when wood is sawn or burned, and could also leach into acidic soil or acid rain. Although the use of this type of wood may be inviting, especially for its longevity, it would be better to use normal wood, especially for flower beds for the growth of plants intended for food consumption, changing it completely every 5 years.

New treated wood does not contain arsenic. However, recycled wood may have traces of it.

CHAPTER 10
DESIGN OF A FLOWER BED

O rganizing the spaces in the garden is useful for optimizing it: if you plan well, the plot will be comfortable to work with and at the same time make the most of its size. Before preparing the land and sowing it, it is worth drawing a map of the garden and deciding how to divide it into flower beds.

The flower beds will be divided by walkways, which in addition are useful for moving around the field, without ever stepping on cultivated land. Giving each element the right size is very important, to allow comfortable work without ever having to walk on the plots.

The size of the flower beds

It is important to establish the dimensions of the various elements, without forgetting to provide service spaces, such as a tool shed, rainwater collection, compost heap. The basic unit is obviously the cultivated bed.

I hypothesize to make rectangular flower beds: it is the best way to use the space. Or you can divide the field as if it were a grid, with walkways parallel or perpendicular to each other.

The flower beds must be made up to a maximum width of 120 cm, which allows work to be carried out inside, without having to climb onto the cultivated land. In fact, a space of just over a meter can be reached easily if it has walkways on both sides. The length of the flower bed can instead be established at will, although it is practical not to exaggerate with the length and create a greater number of links in which to walk.

It may be worth raising the flower beds with respect to the passageways, this offers several advantages in terms of cultivation, as we have detailed.

In the synergistic vegetable garden, circular or spiral flowerbeds / pallets are sometimes created that come out of these schemes, very aesthetically beautiful creations. This type of design must necessarily be customized to each space and lends itself little to a general discourse. In any case, the width of 120 cm should be respected even on these eccentric beds.

Since often the direction of the flowerbed also determines the orientation of the rows, for convenience and better use of the spaces, it is good to remember during the design phase that having the rows of vegetables oriented east-west can mean better lighting for the plants, which there will be less shade between them. It is not easy to explain it in words, but if you observe which way the shadow is oriented during the day you will know.

The width of the walkways

The walkway is the space that divides one flower bed from the others, at the same time they are the streets where those who cultivate walk to cross the garden. The width of this passage must be sufficient to pass comfortably, at the same time it must not be exaggerated, because the passages are unproductive spaces.

A good width could be 35/40 cm if it is a small vegetable garden managed with manual tools. If, on the other hand, we want to pass between the flower beds with a wheelbarrow or a rotavator, it is good that the spaces are adequate and the walkways can even exceed 50 cm.

If we want a compromise we can make some walkways of greater width, the "main arteries" and they will allow us to pass with the aforementioned wheelbarrow or rotavator, while others we keep tight and will only be used by those who cultivate to pass on foot.

For convenience, we can decide to mulch the walkways using straw, sawdust or cardboard, but also pave them with boards or sand. On the one hand, this prevents walkers from getting their feet too dirty, and does not allow weeds to grow in the passages.

Draw straight walkways

It seems like an exaggerated stinginess but I assure you that it is worth getting a wire and a few pegs, to accurately trace the borders of the flower beds and create a regular garden, made of parallel lines and angles always at 90 degrees. If you dig passages by eye, without a measured and stable reference, you end up with crooked lines, which results in the non-use of small parts of arable land.

Obviously, a perfectly rectangular plot is not always available, so there will be flower beds in the shape of a triangle or trapezoid at the edges, with some sides a bit crooked, it is inevitable.

Raised beds are very useful as they ensure a bountiful harvest. You can decide to design the flower bed according to your ideas and needs or buy a pre-assembled one.

A raised flower bed enriches your garden. Whether you decide to use it to plant lots of colorful flowers or as a small vegetable garden, the raised flowerbed is always an eyecatcher in the garden - especially if it's DIY and made from recycled materials such as discarded doors or pallets. In addition, it makes gardening work much easier: when you take care of the plants, in fact, you do not have to stay all the time in an awkward position with a hunched back.

Of course you can grow your favorite plants, however its main purpose lies at the forefront of growing vegetables and herbs. The multi-layered structure, enriched with organic waste from the garden, promises a particularly abundant harvest. A further advantage is also given by its shape: the height and the external material of the raised bed offer natural protection from attack by snails. Flowers and vegetables, almost unreachable by these voracious parasites, are therefore safe.

In principle, you will need a frame of about 80-90 cm in height that you will anchor firmly in the ground and which, later, you will fill with various layers of soil and compost. Those who dabble in DIY and have the right equipment can choose the material that best suits their garden and, with minimal effort, build a raised bed with their own hands. Here's what you need:

Material and work tools

Tightly woven wire mesh

Sheet for ponds or special thermal bubble film

Compost and soil for plants and flowers

Building a do-it-yourself raised bed has the advantage of being able to create completely customized shapes using the most varied materials so that the flower bed is in perfect harmony with the rest of the garden. Do you want a simpler and more immediate solution? No problem, we have one that's right for you. With ready-made assembly kits or pre-assembled models, building a raised bed becomes child's play.

Design and preparation work of the raised flowerbed

The search for suitable material begins. Wood, stone, synthetic material, metal, unused pallets or even bamboo: for your DIY raised flowerbed you can indulge yourself in the choice of material. Some materials, such as coir mats for example, decompose naturally and therefore only last a few years. However, given that the raised bed will still need to be refilled approximately every five years, you can possibly take advantage of the opportunity to build a new one. A separate discussion should be made for raised brick flower beds or gabions filled with natural stones.

The height should be around 80cm. As for the shape, however, we advise you not to go too deep so that you can comfortably reach all the points when managing and caring for the plants. If you decide to opt for a ready-made assembly kit, clearly you won't have to worry about taking the measurements: just follow the instructions and proceed directly with the assembly.

Building a raised bed: DIY instructions

1

Prepare the ground

Once you have chosen where to place the bed, remove the turf and about 10 cm of the top layer of earth, fix the anchors of the bed. If you create a masonry or natural stone flower bed ENSURE THE STABILITY OF THE SOIL.

2

Building the walls

Now you can dedicate yourself to the realization of the external structure of the flower bed. If you're building with pallets, stack them on top of each other on the long side, then join them by screwing them together at the corners. The bottom of the pallets must face outwards so that the internal surface of the bed is homogeneous. The advantage of building a flower bed with pallets? Once the flower bed is ready, you can use the grooves, facing outwards, embellishing them with potted plants or even closing the bottom and planting decorative plants directly.

3

Protect the ground

Palette, reclaimed wood, stone: regardless of the material you will use to build the flower bed, the soil protection technique does not change. To protect the bed from voles, cover the still uncovered ground with a tightly meshed wire mesh, leaving about 10-20 cm more on each side that you will firmly attach to the walls.

4

Cover the internal walls

Line the inside walls (not the floor!) Of the flower bed with pond tarp or special bubble wrap. This protects the material from moisture and the soil from drying out, producing the heat necessary for decomposition.

Fill the bed with several layers and plant the plants

Finally, fill the flower bed by creating several layers of garden waste, soil for plants, compost and soil for flowers and, at the appropriate time, proceed to sowing or planting the plants.

Warm bed box or movable raised bed? With DIY everything is possible!

The flowerbed is not only extremely fertile thanks to the stratification and guarantees rather abundant harvests: with the suitable hot bed box, sowing and harvesting can already be carried out a few weeks before or after the actual season.

The do-it-yourself raised flowerbed does not find its place only in the garden: it is in fact an ideal decorative element also for balconies and terraces. The choice of a do-it-yourself flower bed, in this case, is even more appropriate to make the most of the spaces, which are in themselves limited. If your balcony is particularly small you will have to rely on creativity. For example, you can get some tall plant containers and turn them into a raised bed. Tubs or buckets with wheels are the ideal solution: they are easy to move, so you can move them at will so that your plants can enjoy the sunlight to the maximum. But you can also mount wheels on a large raised bed for the roof terrace - as long as they are suitable for the weight. And here's a DIY mobile raised bed ready.

CHAPTER 11
CHOOSING THE PLACE FOR YOUR RAISED BED

How to find the right location.

A raised flower bed offers many benefits. One of them, for example, is that you can start earlier with sowing and planting plants, thus protecting them more from pests. But at the moment of realization it is important to observe some aspects, in particular the position.

There tend to be several places in which to place the raised flower bed: the garden, the terrace, but also the balcony or the greenhouse. If possible, in most cases we opt for the garden. This, in fact, is the ideal place as it offers the optimal conditions for the growth, care and watering of your plants. Furthermore, usually in the garden there is more space available than on the balcony or terrace, which is why you can indulge yourself in the choice of shape and size. The optimal measures are 2 m in length, from 80 to 100 cm in height and 80 cm in width: these dimensions, in fact, allow you to comfortably reach all areas of the flower bed. Rectangular flower beds are usually the most practical, especially at the time of sowing and harvesting.

North-South: perfect orientation

If possible, you should orient it in a north-south direction to ensure optimal light exposure for your plants. Whether you decide to plant vegetables, herbs or flowers, it makes no difference: the north-south orientation is ideal for most plants. Also, if it is in the garden, avoid placing it in the shade of tall plants such as trees, hedges or bushes, which steal precious light from the seedlings and hinder their growth. Furthermore, it is important to distribute the plants according to their height to prevent them from stealing light from each other: climbing plants and flowers should be planted on the side facing north, while on the side facing south, plants that don't grow tall should be placed.

Tip: herbs grow best on the edges. Additionally, we recommend that you place the raised bed near a water source to save time and labor when watering.

The raised flowerbed on the terrace and balcony

When the flowerbed is placed in the garden it is in direct contact with the ground. This, of course, is impossible on a balcony or terrace. Raised flower beds for terraces or balconies offer plants conditions similar to those in pots, and above all the possibilities for storing water are limited. For this reason, they are ideal for creating a herb garden: basil, parsley, rosemary and thyme grow luxuriantly on the terrace or balcony. For aesthetic reasons, many choose to place the raised flowerbed next to garden chairs or sofas: especially if it hosts beautiful flowers, it becomes a delicate decorative element that certainly does not go unnoticed.

Orientation is decisive

Do not forget, however, that the position of the balcony or terrace itself affects the good growth of the plants: if these are oriented to the south and therefore very sunny, we recommend that you opt for Mediterranean plants such as sage, thyme, lavender and rosemary. If the balcony or terrace, on the other hand, is oriented to the north, you will have to choose plants that do not need too much light, for example aconite, bluebell, glass flower and fuchsia. Based on the exposure of the place where you want to place the flower bed and doing a little research you will find the plants that are right for you.

The raised bed in the greenhouse: optimal protection from bad weather

The greenhouse also lends itself perfectly to hosting your raised bed. Being a closed place, the plants find themselves in completely different climatic conditions. Here the plants are protected from the elements and can thrive. The greenhouse is perfect for growing spinach and salad, which are particularly sensitive to cold, which can be sown, harvested and then enjoyed ahead of time.

CHAPTER 12
PROPERLY FILL A RAISED BED WITH VEGETABLES, FLOWERS, OR HERBS

Preliminary reflections

Decorative or useful plants: each plant has different needs regarding water, light and nutrition. For this we advise you to choose the plants according to the position of your propagation box. Some flowers prefer the penumbra for their growth, while others tolerate only sunny positions. Many plants also last only one year, so you have to respect the right sequence. Regarding the need for nutrients, gardeners distinguish between heavy consuming plants, medium consuming plants and light consuming plants. Heavy consuming plants should be planted in a newly built raised bed as the fresh soil is still rich in nutrients. In the years to come, heavy consuming plants can be replaced with those with reduced nutrient requirements.

Make mixed crops. The cultivation of different varieties promotes growth and increases resistance. Because as a protection from parasites some plants give off fragrances and other substances. Thus, for example, chervil removes snails, lice and powdery mildew making the use of chemical pesticides unnecessary.

Pay attention to a good "neighborhood": a careful choice of plants prevents them from depriving each other of nourishment. In a good mixed crop, plants grow that absorb nutrients in different quantities from the soil and even return some of them. The courgette, a strong consuming plant, goes perfectly with onions or green beans, for example.

Plants that love humidity and those that are sensitive to water do not coexist.

Which plants are suitable?

All plants that require little space and that can withstand even stagnation of water after a heavy rain are suitable. On the other hand, varieties whose strongly branched roots penetrate deeply into the soil are less suitable. A raised bed full of tall, broad-growing decorative plants is soon overflowing and the substrate is no longer sufficient for its needs. Also beware of climbing plants. Very often the height of a crate is insufficient for hanging branches and the stems of climbing plants need a stake as well as a good position protected from the wind.

As a rule, they can be grown more densely than at ground level. Leave enough room for branches, leaves and roots to grow. When planting plants, ensure a favorable arrangement. Plant the tall growing varieties in the center so that they don't detract from other plants. For the sides and edges of the raised bed, choose smaller or climbing plants.

Varieties with a different growth cycle are also recommended for growing raised beds. The "hunt" for water during the flowering of plants will therefore be greatly reduced. In addition, you will have the flowers in bloom at different times and / or provide for the harvest several times a year.

Enrich the soil with suitable nourishment

Decisive for success is a multilayer system. For this it is essential to fill with different substrates. Part of it should be filled with composting material such as garden and kitchen waste. This ensures the supply of nourishment, releases heat through decomposition and ensures a soil with ideal temperatures. Each layer must be between 10 and 25 cm thick. Here's the perfect fill of a raised flower bed:

The lower layer of expanded clay or gravel acts as drainage and prevents water stagnation.

Compostable waste such as shredded material or twigs form the second layer.

The composting material is covered with a thin layer of special soil for raised beds. So you don't have to worry about composting. The substrate is readily available in sufficient quantities, can be filled quickly and is more responsive to the special nourishment requirements within the flower bed. The special soil is suitable for all crops.

A further layer of composting material follows.

Finally, cover everything with a layer of garden soil.

Adapt the filling to plant varieties. The common universal soil is made up of recycled substances, limestone and fertilizers. Some soils also contain bark and bark mulch in varying amounts. Especially with regard to heavy consumer plants, it is advisable to fill the raised bed with substrates that have a high percentage of plant residues of this type. For aromatic herbs, on the other hand, too high a nutrient content is not recommended.

For the planting of seedlings in the flower bed, in addition to the universal soil we also recommend the use of a sowing soil. This has a particularly fine structure and its nitrogen content is reduced due to the different nutritional requirements of the slender seedlings and, in addition, it contains phosphate and potassium.

Miniature vegetable garden - plant suitable varieties in the raised bed

You can start planting suitable varieties. Onions, carrots and cucumbers from your own miniature garden are free from harmful substances and tastier than products from the supermarket.

The most suitable varieties are leafy vegetables, cabbage, bulbous and root vegetables such as field salad, kohlrabi, garlic or radishes. These varieties are of low growth and have flat roots. This is why they are also suitable for small boxes and allow you to set up several units at a time.

When it comes to vegetables, a mixed crop can also work wonders. Tomatoes go perfectly with carrots, leafy salads, cauliflower and spinach, but less so with potatoes, peas and cucumbers. In the first year the flower bed can be filled with strong consuming plants. For example onions, leeks, aubergines and celery. Medium consuming plants such as peppers, radishes, spinach or beetroot will follow. From the third year, the nutrient content is sufficient for green beans, peas and field salad.

For a mixed crop, different plant varieties with smaller fruit are also suitable, such as strawberries. However, these are not compatible with the cabbage varieties.

Raised bed for herbs and salads

Leaves for fresh salads

Leaf salads These are compact plants whose roots grow only a few centimeters underground. The head of the lettuce forms a dense rosette and has a low growth height, so can be planted in the flowerbed, one next to the other. Most varieties prefer a sunny position and should be wintered in the greenhouse. Alternatively, cover them with a protective sheet for plants. The more "herbaceous" spinach, which reaches a growth height of only 10 cm, should not be placed side by side with beets, but with radishes and carrots.

Organic aromatic herbs for tasty dishes

Since some varieties are very delicate, respect for water and nutrition needs is essential for a raised bed for aromatic herbs. Mediterranean herbs prefer a dry location, while sage, lavender, rosemary and thyme should preferably be grown not with other aromatic herbs as they prefer substrates that are poor in nutrition.

A good combination for mixed crops is leafy salads with dill, chives and chervil. High-growing plants such as lovage, tarragon or rosemary should be placed in the center. On the edges plant parsley, cress or chives.

Lush flowering in the raised flower bed.

A flower bed enlivens a bare terrace and embellishes an empty corner. The raised position of the flowers catches the eye.

In addition to decorative plants, useful varieties such as edible nasturtium and sunflowers are also suitable. For flowers it is even more important to take into account the different growth heights. To highlight all the flowers, at the time of planting it is necessary to keep the necessary distance and arrange the long-stemmed flowers in the center. The overall picture is more harmonized if the climbing varieties are placed on the sides. For lush growth, we recommend choosing varieties that bloom at the same time. For a flower bed all year round use varieties with different growth cycles.

Tulips and sunflowers are strong consuming plants, dahlias, pansies and primroses have a reduced need for nutrients. It is equally important to combine the individual colors of the flowers well.

Each type of plant has its own particular preferences in terms of light. Some feel more comfortable in a warm and sunny place, while others prefer a bright place.

Shade is not the same as shadow.

It is still possible to plant many vegetables in light shade, for example:

Many types of cabbage, for example kohlrabi and kale

Salads (valerian, rocket, Asian salads such as pak choi)

Leafy vegetables such as spinach, chard, rhubarb)

Beans green beans, and peas

Broccoli, cauliflower

With many of the vegetables mentioned, however, the yield should be expected to be lower than from a sunnier location.

In the shade, horticultural plants still thrive, such as:

Rocket

Chicory lettuce (for example endive)

Other classic leaf lettuces

Spinach and Swiss chard

Green boys, Brussels sprouts

Advice

Fruits, especially red fruits or early ripening apples and pears, can also be grown in light shade in the beginning. However, due to the lack of sun, the fruits will not be as sweet as in a sunnier location. Exception: typical berries such as wild strawberries also thrive very well in a shaded raised bed.

CHAPTER 13
PLANT THE RAISED BED IN THE FALL

The right moment

The moment to create the flower bed is decisive for the success of your harvest.

Before sowing and harvesting, it is necessary to prepare the raised bed in order to plant aromatic herbs, vegetables or flowers. Cover the ground with a tight mesh grill to keep moles and other animals away. Cover with a layer of coarse components such as chopped twigs and shredded bushes for good aeration. For planting, then overlap vegetable waste, garden soil, compost and precious soil for flowers. This clever layered system creates ideal conditions for the soil and its composition can be adapted to the selected plants. Already at the time of preparation it is advisable to know whether you want to plant decorative or useful plants.

The gardening season begins in spring, but there are already many jobs in the garden in spring. So why not take advantage of the autumn? In this period the gardens are emptied, the garden prepares for hibernation.

Why prepare the flower bed in the fall?

There is a lot of compostable material, useful for the layered construction of the flower bed.

The soil has plenty of time during the winter to settle and the first microorganisms can settle. In a raised bed immediately cultivated it can happen that due to the laying of the soil, inevitable for the decomposition process (every year from 10 to 20 cm), the young roots are damaged.

The raised bed is immediately ready for planting in spring.

In summary, we note that much of the sowing and harvesting period in the raised bed falls in the period between February and October and that this period varies due to the higher and faster harvest than that expected for sowing and harvesting in traditional flower beds. Each plant has its own needs.

One thing is certain: to get a good harvest it is crucial to choose the right moment for sowing. The information can be found on the relevant seed packets. Much more important than strictly sticking to the recommended period is to wait for suitable weather conditions. Avoid planting seeds in cold, wet soil. As temperatures rise, the "delays" are quickly recovered.

When to plant what kind of vegetables?

For those new to growing vegetables in a raised bed, we recommend sticking to the following 5-year plan.

In the 1st year, first plant the so-called heavy consuming plants such as cabbage, onions, cucumbers, tomatoes, carrots or leeks. These are plants with a high nutritional requirement that will receive what is necessary given the still very high concentration of nutrients in the fresh raised bed.

In the 2nd and 3rd year it is up to the medium consuming plants such as spinach, radish, dill and potatoes.

In the 4th and 5th years, we switch to weak consuming plants such as Brussels sprouts, white cabbage, salad, cauliflower or green beans.

As a rule, the nutrients are exhausted after 5 years and the soil must be replaced completely. The old potting soil can be used as humus. In autumn, fertilization with a green fertilizer is recommended.

Harvest time

Cauliflower seedlings, starting from mid-April. 8 to 12 weeks after mass, before the opening of the covering leaves (from August to October).

Broccoli, from January to August when the buds are well formed but still closed.

Dwarf beans, beginning of May (they grow only with temperatures above 12 degrees) about 2 to 3 months after sowing (August).

Peas, from March to July (soil temperature above 8 degrees) after 3 to 4 months (when you can feel the seeds in the shell).

Curly endive, July to September About 8 to 10 weeks later. Resistant to frost, which is why it can be planted even in winter.

Cabbage, from mid-July to early August. Early varieties from September. Resistant to frost, which is why it can be planted even in winter.

Carrots, from March to June. Depending on the variety 4 to 7 weeks after sowing.

Potatoes, depending on the variety from March to May (preparations for planting potatoes already begins in winter). September and October (after about 100 days).

Lettuce, between March and May. After about 10 weeks.

Radishes, between March and September. After about 4 to 6 weeks, until the tubers are still small.

Red chard, between March and August. 3 to 4 months after sowing (at the latest October and November).

Spinach, from February to May. Depending on the variety 10 to 12 weeks after sowing.

Tomatoes, in May, when the frost has passed until late August. Tomatoes harvested in the fall that are still green can ripen indoors (in the dark).

Onions, onion bulbs between February and April. With leaves and dry weather (starting from August).

Flowers are easier to care for than vegetables.

In the first year start with heavy consuming plants such as chrysanthemums, sunflowers, geraniums and tulips, in the second and third year choose medium consuming plants such as snapdragons, dahlias and glossinias and, finally, in the 4th and 5th year weak consuming plants such as azaleas, begonias, petunias, primroses and pansies.

Orient yourself at the time of planting to the flowering period of the individual flowers.

CHAPTER 14
RAISED BEDS

The operation, as it is easy to guess, is useful for creating a functional seedbed and also brings significant benefits to the drainage of the portion of land in which it is performed.

Why raised beds?

Before beginning: evaluate the season, the needs of the soil and your crops.

Before carrying out any operation on the ground, it is necessary to make sure that it can produce real benefits. In fact, hasty decisions are often made, which do not take into account the seasonality, as well as the very characteristics and properties of the soil to be cultivated. With the imminent start of winter, for example, it is essential to make assessments regarding the climatic conditions typical of this period. Rain and frost certainly condition the preparation of the soil for the sowing of products such as asparagus and leafy vegetables, as well as for the transplanting of other types of vegetables.

We have already seen how these beds can have a positive impact on the seedbed and avoid water stagnation. In reality, designing a "raised garden" can ensure the achievement of a large number of advantages, which concern various aspects. Let's find out together, then, some of the main benefits of the bed.

1. Fewer diseases for a more productive harvest

Controlling water drainage allows for a lower risk of diseases for plants. This happens because, thanks to the bed, it is possible to create a free zone for the roots of our plants and for what are defined as root capillaries, but also the right balance between the water and oxygen content of the soil. Furthermore, thanks also to the right amount of water and fertilizers, the bed will benefit from optimal chemical-physical and microbiological conditions, useful for improving the fertility of our plantings.

This optimization, in particular, leads to a tangible increase in production and an increase in the quantity of leaves developed by the cultivated plant, as well as their weight, because raised beds contribute to:

Improve exposure to sunlight

Raising of the soil temperature, with a consequent vegetative restart

Reduce soil compaction

Control of water stagnation

There are also benefits that concern the raised cultivation bed on the root system of plants. This operation, in fact:

Eliminates the risks of water stagnation, radical asphyxia

Creates the right balance between the water and oxygen content of the soil

It reduces the predisposing factors for attacks by harmful organisms

Improves exposure to sunlight

It favors the raising of the soil temperature at the vegetative restart

It optimizes the supply of water, nutrients and disinfectants and disinfestants

It respects the balance of the rhizosphere, the portion of soil near the roots, biologically active

Reduces soil compaction

2. Greater convenience in harvesting

Raising the beds, however, not only produces advantages for the plant and its productivity, but is able to facilitate and make the phases relating to the harvest less tiring. Those who carry out this type of operations, in fact, will be able to collect the fruits or vegetables with less effort, since these will be at a greater height.

3. Protect the environment and your land

This operation has not only positive effects at the production level. Creating a raised bed, for example, allows you to:

Avoid water waste (thanks also to the localized drip irrigation method).

Reduce the level of pollution of agricultural operations, thanks to the optimization of the absorption and assimilation of the products used.

4. More quality at a lower cost

Often, it is led to believe that carrying out this type of gardening can lead to an increase in costs. In reality, although they can increase initial costs, you obtain a higher quality level of crops, with savings in terms of resources and working time.

5. Top results: combine bed formers with mulchers

Finally, if you want to get the most out of your land, we recommend combining the use of bed formers with that of mulchers. By covering the soil with a plastic film, or another type of material (as needed), but leaving room for the plant itself for its natural growth, it is possible to maintain the right level of humidity in the upper part of the soil.

Finally, with the combination of these operations, you will be able to:

Have more control over the soil temperature

Protect the grow space from pathogens, insects and weeds

Perform multiple operations in one step

CHAPTER 15
MULCHING

What is mulching? A word that you may never hear in life, but which, for those involved in natural agriculture, synergistic gardens, permaculture and soil protection, is daily bread, an essential practice, a solution to many evils. Mulching is the covering of the cultivated soil with various materials, natural or artificial and is very useful in the vegetable garden. It is carried out for various reasons and with very different materials.

What mulch is used for

Soil in nature is always mulched, that is, covered. Bare soil, without grass, leaves, other living or decaying material does not exist naturally. If a land is completely bare it is not alive, as happens in the desert or in rocky areas. From this simple observation we understand that if we want to grow our edible plants as naturally as possible we must cover the ground. The cover has many functions: it protects the earth (and its inhabitants) from excessive heat or cold, limits evaporation and therefore keeps humidity for longer, slows the growth of spontaneous plants as it stops the passage of light necessary for their growth, avoids the compaction of the earth when it rains. These are the main reasons why mulching is used, a common practice even in intensive production (perhaps made with synthetic materials), but they are not the most important. The organic matter on the surface nourishes the multiplicity of micro and macro organisms which, with their work, are transformed into food that can be assimilated by plants. In practice, it allows the fertility cycle to take place, without this process the soil would be impoverished until it dies. But that's not all.

You may find it useful: vegetable garden in spring, tips for frosts and droughts.

Organic matter is also a powerful sponge that, when it rains, soaks up water and then releases it slowly, allowing it to reach underground aquifers. Without this mantle, also made of humus and roots, the water would not be able to seep into the earth and would slip away quickly, dragging various elements with it. Thus the earth is impoverished and thus the desert is formed. The flash floods, muddy rivers that flow fast towards the sea, sometimes destroying the works of man and taking lives, would not exist without the transformations that man has brought to the planet over the millennia, especially with agriculture. We cannot imagine returning to a primordial phase of the Earth, nor do we wish for it. But a lot can be done if we understand some essential needs of nature: the ground wants to be covered. So when we look at a beautiful freshly plowed and sown field in which not a blade of grass is seen, neither alive nor dead, we are not admiring the beginning of a new life cycle, but the certain premise of the destruction of the greatest terrestrial heritage, fertile soil suitable for life.

Materials for mulching the vegetable garden

There are many materials that lend themselves to mulching, but there are some that only do damage. I'm talking about mulches made with plastic sheets, which are often not even removed, but crushed at the end of the cycle by plowing it into the soil, which pollutes the earth. Almost all natural and biodegradable materials are fine, from straw to wool, from cardboard to leaves, from wood to grass clippings. There is also live mulch, with the land being sheltered by a young crop that as it grows, provides an extra crop beyond what we are protecting.

Use straw as mulch

With his book, The Straw Revolution, Masanobu Fukuoka reminded the world of the importance of ground cover. For him it is a truly revolutionary act, capable of improving production and saving men a lot of effort. The most popular mulch material is cereal straw, but the choice should depend on what you have available spending the least amount of energy and money.

Spreading straw might seem like a rather insignificant thing, but it is fundamental in my way of growing rice and winter cereals. It is the keystone of everything, of fertility, of germination, of weed control, of protection from sparrows, of water regulation. Both in actual practice and in theory, the use of straw in agriculture is an essential issue. Yet people do not seem to be able to understand it.

Emilia Hazelip - the creator of the synergistic agriculture method, which always involves the use of mulch, lists a long series of materials that can be used. In her book Synergistic Agriculture, the origins, experiences, and practices of Emilia Hazelip can be read:

The thickness of the mulch layer will be adapted to the season and the stage of the garden. In winter it will need to be thicker to conserve heat, avoid frost damage and protect the few species of vegetables that survive the cold. In spring, however, it will be necessary to remove or open the mulch only in the spaces where there are plants.

Hay in the Elementary Garden

It is used to cover the soil with a thick layer of about 20 centimeters, this facilitates both the protection and the regeneration of the soil. Hay being much more biodiverse and rich than straw, with the large quantity and diversity of seeds and organic matter, guarantees a greater supply of "nutrients" to the soil.

List of materials for mulching:

Straw

Hay

Leaves

Cardboard and paper

Weeds and shredded prunings

Wool

Remains of winemaking

Bark and sawmill waste

Chopped prunings

Sheep wool mulch

How much mulch should I put in the soil?

The quantity to be spread on the ground varies according to the material chosen. For mulch you can use straw, wheat or other cereals, grass clippings, to be dried before use, reeds, which must be chopped, leaves (excluding those of eucalyptus and pine needles which, however, strawberries like; those of chestnut, walnut and oak are good only if mixed with others), sawdust, but only after a year of aging on the ground, cardboard and paper, even newspapers cut into strips, brushwood and pruning, remains of vinification, goose feathers and sheep's wool.

Live mulch for the soil

To keep the land covered, you can choose to sow grass or alternate crops without the ground having to remain uncovered between one and the other. Like the other types of mulch, it lets us contain overly invasive wild herbs and will help maintain fertility. The father of natural farming, Masanobu Fukuoka suggests using white clover to be sown alongside grains to keep weeds in check. Clover is also a nitrogen fixer and therefore enriches the soil for the benefit of our main crop.

Coffee grounds for mulching

Coffee grounds can also be used for mulching, the important thing is to mix the coffee powder with other materials. The pH of the coffee grounds will be almost neutral, because after the treatment and the boiling it loses most of its acidity. In any case, to avoid plant problems, also due to the presence of caffeine, it is best to use it in moderation.

CHAPTER 16
BUILDING A HEATED CAISSON

To sow vegetables and flowers in advance, you can, with a relatively modest expense, build a heated glass box.

In 1700 a special oak bark chipping was used to keep the plants warm in winter, but fortunately today we can use electricity to warm the box.

You do not need a lot of power, so choose something that keeps the plants warm without cooking them, which develops the heat of a 150 W light bulb.

Arrange it in a serpentine pattern on the bottom of the box, possibly resting on a metal shelf.

The bottom of the box must obviously be completely waterproof, so it is good practice to have it prepared in steel or aluminum by a blacksmith.

The upper part of the box must be made of wood, also waterproofed to prevent the irrigation water from ending up on the wires.

Two coats of galvanized paint will be enough.

For the cover, a glass plate is also sufficient, provided it is very thick to prevent it from cracking or breaking, or even a plexiglass cover, much safer and cheaper, although much less beautiful to look at.

Plexiglass is especially suitable for those who are forced to place the box in a place where it can be reached by dogs or cats, who could break the glass and get seriously injured.

The box must be kept out of the rain as it must be continuously supplied with electricity, but at the same time it must be placed in a bright position.

In case of very heavy rains, isolate it by unplugging it and put it in a plastic bag closed with an elastic band.

Do not put it back into operation if the air is not dry.

The heated box is very useful for sowing especially ornamental plants, which need a long period of acclimatization during the spring, to get to bloom in summer, such as the Thunbergia alata, the Cobaea scadens, Maurandia and some types of Ipomoea, such as the Bonanox species.

CHAPTER 17
CULTIVATION TIPS

Imagine harvesting kilos of tomatoes, immense quantities of eggplant and lots and lots of salad. Yields like these are easier to get than you really think. The secret of a super productive garden is to plan the right strategy and combine it with good organization. Nature has its own rhythms and rules and if we want to eat its fruits we just have to respect them all!

Cultivating the garden means opening a window on nature and its precious teachings. We learn to observe their growth and evolution and to respect the rhythms of the earth, sometimes slow, sometimes incomprehensible, but incredibly fascinating and ancient.

Cultivatinavegetable garden is a hobby, of course, but if we want to achieve good results it takes commitment and also the right knowledge of the fundamental elements.

Light, which must never be lacking in the garden because plants need at least 7 hours a day to bear fruit.

The soil, which must always be well drained, rich in organic substances and protected from dangerous stagnation of water.

Water, an indispensable element, to be managed in the best possible way to avoid deficiencies but also excesses.

Learning everything immediately is practically impossible, but what we can do is learn a little at a time, making use of some small and indispensable tricks that prove to be particularly useful especially if we are beginners.

1. A good raised bed saves your life… and the harvest!

All experienced growers agree on this: soil preparation is the most important factor in increasing yields. A deep, well-nourished and organic soil is able to promote the growth of healthy and extensive roots capable of reaching more nutrients and more water. The result: the soil is more productive and the harvest increases.

The fastest way to get that deep layer of fertile soil is to create raised beds. This is because raised beds produce up to four times more than crops planted in rows.

They also save you time. The plants grow close enough to get rid of any weeds that always form in the garden. Plus, the close planting makes irrigation and harvesting more efficient.

2. Round off the shape of the raised bed

This space becomes more space efficient if you gently round the ground to form a sort of mound. It sounds nonsense, but it's nonsense that can really make a big difference in terms of the total planting area.

A mound of soil in the middle will help you extend the planting area, saving you valuable space. Plants like spinach and lettuce will thank you!

3. No more rows, from now on to plant in triangles!

But what does it mean? It means that to get the most out of each bed, you need to pay attention to how you organize your plants. Avoid planting in square or row patterns. Plant in triangles.

Just be careful to space the plants well. Some plants will not reach their full size - or yield - if the space is too crowded. For example, do you know that if you increase the distance between the lettuces, the weight of the crop increases?

Too tight spacing can also put stress on plants, making them more susceptible to disease and insect attack. Remember that!

4. Grow vertically

If you plant vertically you will have more space. Grow tomatoes, peas, squash and melons in this way; let them grow straight up, supported by trellises, fences and pegs.

Vertical cultivation of vegetables also saves time. Harvesting and maintenance will be faster because you will be able to see exactly where the vegetables to be harvested are. Fungal diseases are also less likely to affect upward growing plants due to improved air circulation around the foliage.

5. Beware of associations!

Deciding to grow compatible vegetables also saves space. Native Americans used the "three sisters" rule; corn, beans and squash. The corn supported the beans, while the squash could grow freely in the soil below, protecting the soil from weeds.

Among the most compatible combinations are tomatoes with basil and onions, lettuce leaves with peas and carrots with radishes. Beets get along well with celery. These rules are the basis of intercropping, because vegetables are just like us in this: they cannot get along with everyone!

6. Plan crops

Sowing in succession allows you to obtain more than one crop in a given space during the same growing season. This way, you can have three or even four crops from a single area. For example, follow a lettuce crop with fast-ripening corn, then grow more vegetables. To get the most you can:

Use transplants. A transplant is already about a month old and matures much faster.

Choose fast-ripening varieties.

Replenish the soil with a good layer of compost.

7. Protect raised beds

Adding a few weeks to the end of the growing season can buy you enough time to grow some more in succession - let's say the time it takes to grow more lettuce or to harvest more tomatoes before the end of summer.

To get these "extra weeks" of production, you will need to keep the air around the plants warm even when it starts to get cold, using sheets and mulch.

You can also use two sheets - one to heat the air and one to warm the ground.

Cover the bed with pitted clear plastic, arrange the plants and cover with straw. Remove the plastic when the air temperature warms up and any danger of frost has passed. Repeat again when temperatures drop.

8. Exposure and location

The ideal vegetable garden is the one kissed by the sun's rays for most of the day, let's say for at least seven hours. It is therefore never grown on the north side of a house or in an area that remains in full shade for most of the day.

Remember that the plants, if they are too crowded, will struggle to grow well and, consequently, will not be productive. In particular, plants that grow very high, such as tomatoes, beans and cucumbers, could, over time, become a kind of barrier from the sun for the lower species, which would not receive the right amount of light.

Lettuce, spinach, radish, rocket, but also cabbage, kohlrabi and parsley can grow without problems even alongside more vigorous and late plants, since they will complete their life cycle before being able to undergo the negative effects of competition for light.

There you have it, have you carefully memorized all these rules? If something has gone wrong so far, start all over again, and ... good cultivation!

CHAPTER 18
GROWING IN WINTER

Before growing winter vegetables in a raised garden, you need to ask yourself a very important question: are you more for a DIY raised garden or willfrom you buy specialized shops? The selection of already complete raised gardens is large. If you prefer to make your own, you will find tons of instructions on the Internet that will guide you step by step. In any case, remember it is important to line the raised garden with bubble wrap before filling it.

Protection from cold and humidity

Thanks to the layered structure and slowly decaying raw materials, heat is created in the raised garden. Unfortunately, this is not always sufficient protection against humidity or cold. So you should consider taking additional measures. For this purpose, polyethylene roofs or tunnels are suitable, with which it is possible to further protect the planting from adverse conditions. Always remember that plants breathe, so you should leave the covers open at least on the sides during the day so that the plants get enough oxygen.

Cold-resistant winter vegetables

Typical winter vegetables must be planted as early as May to harvest between November and February. During the harvesting phase it is also important to pay attention to frosts. When harvesting vegetables, make sure they are sheltered, otherwise the frost will damage the taste. (Except Brussels sprouts, which become less bitter). Salad varieties that also like low temperatures include spinach, leeks and radishes.

In spring it is time to harvest what is left of the previous year. Although no longer edible, what is left over is ideal as a fertilizer. If the substrate level of the raised garden has dropped, simply add some soil. Over time, a relatively solid soil structure with stable microflora will develop. Once you have fertilized with winter waste and added new soil, your garden is ready to welcome new crops!

CHAPTER 19
BUILDING A RAISED BED ON A BALCONY

In fashion now on city terraces and balconies, it represents the most immediate method for cultivating a small personal garden. The raised garden really has numerous advantages.

It might seem that the raised garden is a recent invention. In reality it has very ancient medieval origins that date back to the French, German and Italian monasteries where this type of vegetable garden was intimately connected to the garden.

It could also seem that its main purpose is to facilitate the work by raising the ground level to disprove the famous saying "the land is low". The monks decided to adopt this technique to conserve heat in order to prolong the growing season of fruit and vegetables. In those days, products such as fresh manure were used which, inside the box, fermented, improving the local microclimate. Today this purpose has certainly taken a back seat and, indeed, fresh organic products are no longer used for garden fertilization.

But there is no doubt that this solution is excellent for facilitating cultivation even today as it favors weed control and reduces the possibility of pathogens attacking crops. A container cultivation allows you to mix the optimal growing medium and, if necessary, to replace an exhausted one.

At one time these boxes were made with intertwined willow branches, then we moved on to wood and, in modern times, to more contemporary materials. For example, there are canvas containers that open thanks to the tension caused by the presence of the soil, while in certain contexts it could be interesting to build containers in bricks (remember that porous stones will tend to lose heat much faster).

Even the use of industrial pallets, now in vogue, is interesting above all because these objects can be placed both horizontally and vertically. However, it is a recycled material not designed for this purpose and therefore does not optimize the available space. Indeed, this aspect is one of the determinants of contemporary raised gardens: unlike medieval monasteries, the space available is really limited and, therefore, must be exploited to the fullest. Plastic containers are therefore welcome as long as they are well-made, resistant to bad weather and, above all, to ultraviolet rays which tend to "cook" low quality ones.

The main feature of the raised garden is the fact that the structure of the flowerbed is not located at ground level but is at a variable height. This method gives us the possibility to manage a more orderly vegetable garden but above all to cultivate the vegetable garden even on not very fertile and stony soils, even on the terrace.

To raise the flower bed you can use staves, pallets, wooden boards, sheet metal bands or boxes that will act as containment to the cultivation soil. I chose to build my garden with pallets. Let's get to work right away and let's get busy!

WHAT IS NEEDED:

Pallet

Drill or hammer

Screws or nails

Medium coarse sandpaper

Topsoil

Plants or seedlings to sow

Waterproof fabric (cellophane)

We take our pallet and remove all the planks, being careful of nails and splinters. We will use the wood obtained and assemble it to build our raised beds.

The planks I pulled out of my pallet had a width of about 7.5cm and a length of 86cm. By placing them side by side, I created a height of 15cm and I decided to build two rectangular beds 86cm wide, 15cm high and 20cm deep. Once the two beds are built, we will fix them on top of each other to develop our vegetable garden's height.

We take some medium sandpaper and slowly begin to sand all the parts before assembling them, in such a way as to make the surface very smooth and linear, free of possible elements that could cause damage while we are working.

We are now ready to create our beds! First I created a base of 86x20cm for each. To create the long side of the bed I used 86cm boards and fixed them at the ends with screws using a piece of board 15cm high to get the desired height. I fixed the long sides to the base with screws and then I added the short side by cutting the boards to the necessary width (net of the thickness of the long boards and the vertical plug that holds them fixed).

At this point we need to build our support. Just use two vertical boards and fix perpendicularly to a shorter board which will rest on the floor and act as a support "foot".

We remove any nails that may be present and make sure there are no splinters. Let's sand each part again to be sure that the surfaces are very smooth. We can decide whether to leave our garden natural or personalize it by using a coat of water-based paint, in order to give color to the bed.

We assemble the pieces by fixing the two beds on top of each other along the vertical axes that will support them.

Once the structure has been created, make sure it is stable, take a waterproof fabric and position it with the help of a stapler, so that it will adhere to the base of the pallets. In this way we will have created the bag that will contain the soil, compost and peat of our DIY garden.

With a nail or a thin screwdriver, we drill small holes in the base to allow excess water to escape and thus prevent mold or rot.

The earth will have to be leveled, but make sure that it does not come out completely. We also put some natural fertilizer, such as manure. My advice is to plant rosemary, mint, peppermint, chilli pepper, basil or salad plants, because they are plants that will give life to a vegetable garden that is truly envied by the neighbors. The earth will give us many delights, completely natural and also free of chemical fertilizers and pesticides!

If we wanted, we could also make small plywood signs, enameled with blackboard paint, with the name of the plant that we placed in that particular position written on it, so as not to make mistakes.

We also offer you a much faster method:

Needed:

1 wooden box (you can get it from your greengrocer)

Yute cloth

1 plastic sheet

Expanded clay

1 bag universal soil

Seedlings of your choice

Method:

1 Cover the base of the wooden box with the jute cloth. Then

insert the plastic sheet inside the box above the jute sheet.

2 Now you can fix the sheets on the box with a simple nail or staple gun. Drill some holes in the bottom of the box so as not to allow water to stagnate and allow the soil to drain properly.

3 Now you can put the expanded clay in the box and immediately put the soil on top.

4 Choose the plants (for example, basil goes well with tomatoes) and let them soak in water for a few minutes in order to be ready for transplanting.

5 With a trowel dig a hole in the soil of the box (preferably towards the center)

6 Insert the plants you have previously chosen inside

7 Place the box on your balcony, taking care to place it in the sun and water it regularly (preferably in the evening or away from the hottest hours).

CHAPTER 20
6 RULES FOR A GARDEN ON THE BALCONY

Many wonder if it is possible to cultivate a real vegetable garden on a balcony or terrace, without having to limit oneself to the cultivation of ornamental plants and flowers. My answer is usually yes, at least within certain limits and with due precautions.

1. The choice of containers

Before planning your home production of vegetables, you must check that the terrace can support the weight of the earth and the pots: in general, we are talking about a maximum of 350 kg of load per square meter. This element - together with the expense factor - will condition the choice of the quantity and type of containers to be prepared, which must be about 40 cm deep (but 20cm are enough for cutting salads): in fact, for the health of the plants, large pots in porous terracotta are the most suitable and certainly preferable to those made of resin, even if heavier, bulky and therefore also more difficult to move. The depth of the container is obviously affected by the type of vegetable that must grow in it: if the roots of tomatoes are long and need more space, salads have much more limited needs.

There are also very light containers on the market such as fabric bags for cultivation or very pretty containers such as vases in woven willow, but there the expense rises considerably. As an alternative to the aforementioned jars, you could very well recycle from supermarkets a box of similar height, light ones with handles, perforated and made of plastic, for fruit or drinks, filled with a waterproof sheet, on the bottom of which you will have drilled drain holes for water.

Avoid immediately filling your balcony with plants and pots: it is better to have a limited number to take care of to get used to it and then gradually increase the number.

2. The exposition

The garden on a terrace or balcony must face south-east or south-west. Tomatoes, peppers and chillies, aubergines, strawberries and many herbs such as basil, sage, mint, parsley, chives, oregano, rosemary and lavender in fact require full sun for a good part of the day, while the different varieties of lettuce, cut salads, spinach, chard and green beans prefer slightly more shaded corners. With the entry into winter perennials such as aromatic plants must be prepared for the coldest days: place the pots in a corner sheltered from the winds and well exposed to the sun, some of them must be pruned heavily and mulched with straw and leaves, others should be covered with non-woven fabric.

3. What to grow

Each of you lives in different climatic zones, so it is difficult to prescribe a mix of crops truly suitable for all terraces without disregarding the real conditions, exposure as well as practice and experimentation on site: however it is well known that like gardens on the ground, even in the winter period, terraces can give you a harvest of cabbage, rocket and salad, as well as the last strawberries. Chicory and cutting lettuce can share the pot with radishes. There are seeds and seedlings specially selected for vegetable gardens on the market: in general and for all seasons, especially for fruit plants, it is advisable to choose the dwarf varieties, while the cultivation on a terrace of some plants such as potato, onion, carrot or artichoke remains feasible, but certainly more complex (for example, there are now on the market cylindrical columns with double openings, created specifically for potatoes). For reasons of space but also of biological balance, you can follow the method of intercropping plants using the same pot for several complementary varieties (eg strawberries + lettuce). Use a cool corner of the terrace for berries, because they tolerate the cold well; vice versa, potted citrus fruits are very sensitive, they must be protected from the winds and well covered or sheltered during the winter.

4. The soil

To facilitate the drainage of water, prepare a bottom layer of two fingers height of expanded clay or pumice or volcanic lapillus. Use 2/3 excellent quality universal soil combined with 1/3 organic fertilizer or compost of the same quality (if you have not already bought it, if possible, use a composter for composting vegetable residues along with leaves and flowers).

CHAPTER 21
TOP 10 EASIEST VEGETABLES TO GROW ON A BALCONY

Lettuces, of all types

    Zucchini and Cucumbers

    Beets for cutting

    Basil, parsley and rocket

    Carrots and onions

    4 season strawberries

    Tomatoes

    Peppers, even spicy

    Eggplant

    Celery

    Growing lettuce on the balcony

    N ° 1 - Lettuce and baby lettuce:

Orto Mio lettuces can stand the cold and can always be transplanted, even in winter. They are available in "packs" (trays) of 9 plants, in cubes of pressed soil, which favors faster rooting. They are transplanted leaving about 1/3 of the cube out of the ground. In 30/50 days from transplanting, they are ready for harvesting.

They need 10/20 cm deep containers, at least 10 cm wide (geranium boxes are ideal). They benefit from moderate fertilization, with bio-liquid products, 2-3 weeks after transplanting (not necessary if the soil is already fertilized).

Irrigate 1-3 times a week, wetting the soil around the cubes. It is also advisable to wet the cubes if they are very dry.

Among the lettuces, many varieties are ideal for being grown from "lettuce", allowing a very fast harvest, with multiple cuts from the same plants (the first after a week!). They are transplanted without separating the cubes.

Baby lettuce for cutting

The lettuce are identified with a symbol indicated on the left of the boxes.

Lettuces are the ideal plants to be associated with other species.

Grow zucchini on the balcony

N ° 2 - Zucchini and Cucumbers:

Zucchini and cucumbers are vigorous plants, which need containers of 40 cm in diameter and as many in depth. They require very generously fertilized soil and full sun exposure. If transplanted before the end of April, they must be protected with nylon, because they don't like the cold. They require little irrigation in the first 20 days after transplanting and abundant wetting in full production.

Fertilize every 2-3 weeks with organic liquid or granular products, for prolonged production.

Cucumbers can be managed by making them "climb" on a net, on reeds or on a grid.

Courgettes can be tied to a brace on a weekly basis, 40 days from planting. After 25/40 days from transplanting, fruit production will begin (the first may be small and malformed and must be harvested quickly), continuing generously for a couple of months. Then they will have to be replaced with new plants.

Grow chard on the balcony

N ° 3 - Beets for cutting:

They need pots like those of lettuce. They grow well both in the sun and in partial shade, with transplants starting from mid-March. They require moderate fertilization, every 2-3 weeks with organic liquid fertilizer. Water, but avoid stagnation. In 30-50 days after transplanting it will be possible to harvest the chard.

Grow basil, parsley and rocket

N ° 4 - Basil, parsley, rocket, chives:

Basil, parsley, rocket and chives need containers at least 20 cm deep and 10 cm wide. Universal well-drained soil like soil for aromatic plants. Fertilize every 2-3 weeks with organic liquid fertilizer. After 10-15 days from the transplant, the first leaves of basil, parsley and rocket can be harvested. Parsley and chives can be planted as early as February, rocket from March. Basil can be moved outside when temperatures reach 15°C.

Grow carrots and onions on the balcony

N ° 5 - Carrots and onions:

For carrots and onions, containers 20-30 cm deep and 10 wide are needed. Use a light, well-drained and fertilized soil. They can be transplanted as early as February-March. Carefully water to avoid stagnation. Fertilize the onions with organic NPK fertilizer, rich in potassium (K), one month after transplanting and at the beginning of bulbs enlargement. In 50/90 days from transplanting, carrots and onions will be ready for harvesting. They are perfect species to be associated with lettuces.

N ° 6 - 4 seasons Strawberries:

These strawberries do not fear the cold and are transplanted as early as February. Use containers, 20/30 cm deep and the same wide, exposed to the sun or in partial shade. Use a well-drained potting soil or suitable strawberry substrate. Fertilize with NPK fertilizers rich in potassium (K), every 2-3 weeks, in spring. In 50/80 days from transplanting they will produce the first fruits.

Grow tomatoes on the balcony

N ° 7 - Tomatoes:

Tomatoes need pots at least 30/40 cm high and about 40 cm wide, and full sun exposure. Transplant from April on, with generously fertilized soil for vegetables. They require little irrigation in the first 20 days after transplanting and more abundant watering in full production. Tie the stem to a cane, after 20-30 days and remove the female shanks weekly). Fertilize every 2-3 weeks with organic liquid or granular products, for prolonged production. The dwarf varieties should not have the females removed and do not need canes.

After 60/90 days from the transplant, the first fruits will be ripe. Grafted tomatoes guarantee a much higher and continuous production.

Dwarf tomatoes "without cane"

Dwarf tomatoes have a limited development and can be grown even without stakes, or being fixed to canes, to 50-60 cm high.

The most suitable varieties of the range are the Minuet dwarf datterino, the Achico dwarf cherry, the round Bellarosa, the long Enzo and the oval varieties for sauce, Rio Grande Heinz, Big Rio and elongated Incas.

N ° 8 - Peppers, even spicy:

Peppers need containers of 30-40cm in height and width. The soil must be well drained and fertilized very generously. Transplant from the end of April. Carefully avoid water stagnation. They grow well in the sun, but they like a little shade in the hottest hours from July, which will protect them from sunburn. Fertilize every 2-3 weeks with organic granular or liquid fertilizer. Upon reaching 40 cm in height, the stem will be tied to a brace. 50-60 days after transplanting, the first green peppers can be harvested; after 80-90 days the ripe colored fruits. Grafted plants allow earlier and more generous production.

N ° 9 - Aubergines:

Each plant needs containers 30-40 cm deep and about 40 cm wide. Use drained soil, fertilized very generously. Transplant from the end of April. Carefully avoid water stagnation. They love the sun, but they like some shade in the hottest hours from July on. When it reaches 40cm in height, the stem is tied to a brace. Fertilize every 2-3 weeks with liquid or granular bio fertilizer. After 50/80 days from the transplant, the first aubergines will be ready. Collect them as soon as they stop growing, while the skin is still bright (opacity is a symptom of aging which determines an abundance of seeds and a bitter taste). Grafted plants produce earlier and much more generously, even in pots.

N ° 10 - Celery:

Celery needs containers at least 30 cm deep and 20 cm wide. Use a quality soil, well drained and generously fertilized. It likes partial shade, but is also suitable for other exposures (sun and shade). Potted celery is transplanted from the end of March. For rapid development, fertilize every 2-3 weeks with organic liquid fertilizer. In 50/60 days from the transplant, the first sticks can be harvested.

Who is not excited by the idea of going out on their terrace, to pick a ripe tomato, to be consumed immediately at the table? Starting the adventure of the potted garden, it is natural to also think about the possible difficulties that will await us. In reality, most of the time, growing in pots is much easier than doing it in the garden ... as long as you observe a few simple rules!

When can transplanting be started?

The right period for transplanting vegetables depends on the characteristics of the cultivated species (which are more or less resistant to low temperatures), the climate of the growing area and protection against the cold. Production techniques also play a role in obtaining more cold-tolerant seedlings.

Some vegetables can be transplanted as early as the end of winter: lettuce, chard, valerian, parsley, onion, garlic, legumes, artichokes, strawberries, cutting radicchio, etc.

Jars and containers of adequate size

To accommodate the plants, you can choose from pots (of different materials and sizes), to perforated soil bags, wooden crates and inexpensive containers at almost zero cost (such as sturdy sacks, recovery bins and old pots, perhaps coated externally to make them more decorative), to options for "vertical gardens", suitable for species with limited development. It is always necessary that the containers chosen are equipped with holes for the drainage of excess water.

For the health of plants, it is essential that the size of the pot is proportionate to the vigor of the species planted. Too small pots do not allow adequate development of the root system and have a negative impact on production.

The quality of the soil

Choosing the right growing medium is among the key elements to obtain good production. It is always convenient to buy high quality soil (ask your Orto Mio dealer for advice), which guarantees balanced plant growth.

Fertilization

A fundamental factor. A good organic soil, already fertilized, is a good starting point to ensure that each plant has regular development in the first weeks. For short cycle vegetables (lettuce, chard, kohlrabi, parsley, rocket, valerian, radish, etc.) this is sufficient to complete the cycle.

The most demanding species (tomato, pepper, aubergine, cucumber, courgette, etc.), will benefit from nutritional supplements during growth, to best express their productive potential.

Species and exposure

To plan which vegetable species to grow, consider whether they will be able to enjoy sufficient hours of sunshine. If you can choose, avoid spaces in the shade for the whole day, because they preclude the cultivation of many important species such as tomatoes, aubergines, and peppers. But if your passion is lettuce, you can take away some satisfaction, even if the sun's rays do not warm your balcony or your garden.

Arrangement of plants

It is good to carefully plan the spaces to be allocated to the vegetables that must coexist on the same terrace or in a common pot, to avoid creating a jungle, or leaving large areas unused.

The transplant

At transplant, the seedlings face changes, which cause a little initial stress. It is therefore important to put them in the best environmental conditions, so that they can take root quickly. The operation must be carried out at the most favorable moment of the day, to limit the risk of crises due to wind, critical temperatures, etc.

Irrigation

The first irrigation, after the transplant, will be more abundant (and half an hour after the operation, the water left in the saucer must be removed). The frequency and quantity of water introduced will depend on the ambient temperature and on the size of the pots and plants. By controlling the humidity of the soil, before a new watering, errors will be avoided.

Pruning, braces and bindings

"Fruiting" vegetables take advantage of simple operations that can favor their health and production, while at the same time facilitating the management of spaces. Pruning, tying, tutoring, fruit thinning, etc. they are necessary practices in many species grown in pots.

CHAPTER 22
GROWING THE SALAD

Sowing the salad: how, where, when

You can broadcast sow (spreading the seeds by hand) or in rows, along furrows, directly on the ground or even in a seedbed, and then transplant the seedlings, taking care to position the collar (intersection point between stem and roots) to ground level, but not buried. For cutting qualities, spread the seed evenly; for head varieties, sow them in rows about 30-40 centimeters apart.

Starting from the seeds, it will take you about a month longer. Better to bury small plants from your trusted dealer from February / March or at the end of August.

A perhaps little-known technique involves the cultivation of the salad starting from the scraps: you just need to buy a head of lettuce, eliminate the outermost leaves and carve the lower part of the head. Immerse the base of the head for a centimeter in a container or bowl of water and place it in front of a window.

After 15 days you will begin to see the first leaves and roots. Replace the water once a day, then, when the leaves have grown, transplant the head into a pot, with rich soil and put it back in front of the window. The first leaves of this salad will be ready in a few days.

The best time is from February to September. In open ground, it can be sown or planted several times at a distance of 45/60 days (if sown) or two weeks (in the case of transplanting seedlings).

On the balcony, aim for at least 4 seedlings at a time: as they grow you will cut the second and fourth plants, letting the other two grow and replanting two more plants in the empty space again and so on.

The soil suitable for salad

Salad requires a soft, light soil, well drained, rich in nutrients, especially nitrogen: prepare a fertilizer 15 days before transplanting. It needs many hours of sun a day and withstands temperatures that are not too high; it also needs a lot of water every day.

Better to water in the coolest hours, so as not to create a high temperature difference that would be harmful. These precautions also apply to cultivation on the balcony: place the pot in a sunny position, moving it to partial shade in the middle of summer. Alternatively, both in summer and in winter, cover the plants with a veil of non-woven fabric, which will protect them from both excessive heat and cold.

Pay attention to the drainage of the soil.

The salad harvest is not difficult at all: in the cutting varieties, cut the leaves when they are 7 to 10 centimeters high, in those from the head you have to grow them until they are ripe and cut at the root. It goes without saying that the first variety allows more harvests, while the second does not grow anymore.

The enemies of salads and how to defend them

Salads are very resistant: the most frequent danger is represented by snails, which feed on the younger leaves. Different remedies can be used, from snail killers (to be used carefully as they are chemical) to natural remedies such as sprinkling ash or sand around the seedlings or making traps with beer.

If you want organic cultivation, you must provide mulch, natural with straw or artificial with a perforated plastic sheet, a non-woven or biodegradable fabric sheet. With mulching you will solve the problem of weeds and you will have a significant water saving, since the soil will always be moist.

CHAPTER 23
GROWING CUCUMBER

Cucumber is an annual plant which means that once the desired fruits have been given, the soil must be cleaned, which cannot be reused for the cultivation of other cucumbers until after two or three years. Cucumber's favorite soil is well-worked, slightly acidic, and treated with manure a few weeks before planting. With regard to fertilization, in addition to the preventive one we have talked about, it is good to provide fertilizers rich in phosphorus and nitrogen once the seedlings have sprouted and have reached a height of around 15-20 centimeters.

Sowing takes place between April and May. Cucumbers prefer warm climates with constant humidity and love to be close (intercropping) to lettuce, peas, radishes, beans and cabbage; they hate potatoes and aromatic herbs. For sowing, draw rows about 1 meter apart on the cucumber bed. In these rows, at a distance of about 50 centimeters, make small pits about ten centimeters deep and, in each of these put a small amount of manure and three or four cucumber seeds. Once germination has taken place it is important to proceed with the correct thinning: eliminate the less promising plants and leave only the strongest ones.

When germination is advanced, topping must be carried out by pruning the vegetative apex above the fourth leaf and eliminating the lateral shoots. When the plant has reached a height of 20-25 centimeters, it is time to decide whether to let it develop close to the ground in a creeping way or whether to support it for vertical development with a long and sturdy wooden stick (in order to easily support the plant even at the height of its growth). Tie the stem of the plant to the stick with the clamps or the specific wire for this type of intervention so as not to damage the plant. We suggest the vertical development, which is more orderly, easier to manage and more comfortable when harvesting the cucumbers.

Cucumber watering must be frequent, during the days of maximum summer heat every day, taking care to never create stagnant water. The fruit harvest is constant for at least a couple of months. A tip: pick the cucumbers before they have reached their maximum development.

CHAPTER 24
HOW TO REPAIR THE GARDEN ON THE BALCONY FROM SMOG

The main concern is linked to the risk that smog reaches vegetables and greens, settling on them and therefore contaminating the food that then arrives on our tables, considered rightly or wrongly as healthy and natural.

In reality it would be enough to follow a series of precautions to secure our products. It is not that difficult and some precautions are quite easy.

Remember: if you want to be sure of the air quality in your area, the thing to do is to view a certification of the environmental quality of your area.

Tips for protecting an urban garden from smog

First of all, as a first step, we advise you to carefully choose the place to be used for cultivation: fine dust travels for a maximum of 50 meters from the point where it is released and at a very low height, so if the balcony is elevated or is at a greater distance, despite being on the ground floor, you have already eliminated the problem.

Try to change the soil often and use compost in order to eliminate any pollutants and fortify the plants thanks to the very action of renewal.

If you live in a single family house on a busy street, you can buy non-woven fabric, thus covering the entire garden area.

The case of industrial areas

For industrial areas, the problem is a bit thorny: it is very risky to cultivate if you live within a few kilometers of various factories.

Chemical industries in particular may occasionally emit very harmful substances.

In these cases it would be better to resort to different techniques. Among these, we suggest the sprouting or cultivation in covered bins.

Protect an urban garden from smog

Protecting an urban garden from smog is especially important for the health of the little ones.

Wash the vegetables well, always!

Finally, an obvious recommendation, which always holds true. In any case, even if you have put into practice all the useful tips on how to protect an urban garden from smog, never forget to wash the vegetables well.

This is clearly a precaution that also applies to products purchased at the supermarket.

We are often convinced that we are safer with vegetables from the store. Instead, you must not underestimate the exposure of these products to motorway pollution, especially when the products, before arriving in our area, have crossed country traveling on open trucks.

CHAPTER 25
GROWING PARSLEY ON THE BALCONY

Parsley is a biennial plant native to the Mediterranean where it grows spontaneously. To offer its best it needs fertile and well-drained soils, so before sowing it is good to work the soil thoroughly, especially if it is particularly compact, and fertilize it.

You can proceed in early spring, taking care to keep the earth well moist and at a temperature of 18°C. In this way in a fortnight you will see the first shoots, if the temperature is lower the growth will be slower.

After about a couple of months from sowing, you can start the first cuts, taking care to always leave a few centimeters of the stem, so that it can grow back allowing other crops. Parsley grows very fast and therefore allows for several cuts throughout the year. Due to its strong growth it will be necessary to thin it occasionally, leaving about twenty centimeters between one head and another.

Parsley must be eaten fresh. What you will not be able to use fresh, freeze, either in whole leaves or already chopped. Do not dry it because it would lose all its scent.

CHAPTER 26
HOW TO GROW BRUSSELS SPROUTS

How to grow Brussels sprouts: vegetable garden and vase

Brussels sprouts can be harvested from the end of August until February when the early and late species are grown. One plant produces for a long time.

This cabbage (Brassica oleracea var. gemmifera) has a stem 60-80 cm high in the year of sowing and about double in the following year.

In the second year, flower buds develop from the buds and axillary buds of the apical leaves.

To develop, these vegetables need a long season (about 8 months).

Varieties

Among the most cultivated varieties are:

Precocious: Lancelot, Perfection, Long Island.

Intermediate: Prince Askold, Indra.

Late: Sygmund, Jade Cross, Frigostar.

Climate and terrain

Brussels sprouts are plants suitable for cool and humid climates, in fact they prefer summers that are not too hot and with frequent rains. This species is better adapted to the climate of Northern Italy, even pre-Alpine areas, where the heat is often interrupted by summer storms.

Oleracea bullata gemmifera adapts to different exposures and, in areas where there is usually no summer cloud cover, such as in Italy, it is also satisfied with partial shade and, indeed, could be damaged by full sun, if combined with high temperatures and absence of rains.

The ideal soil is the "vegetable garden", fertile, fertilized with mature manure and, above all, well worked up to depth, so that it can be ventilated and drained.

Sowing

The early varieties must be sown under glass in February so that the harvest can be available by the end of August. Spread the seeds sparingly in a bin, in which some grooves 2 cm deep and 15 cm apart have been made. If the rows are too crowded, prune the seedlings. Then proceed to the invigoration.

Sow the intermediate varieties in mid-March in boxes or outdoors, but in a sheltered position. Then proceed with subsequent sowing in a soil suitable for germination, making some furrows 2 cm deep and 15 cm apart. These sowings can continue until mid-April; for the latter use late varieties.

Later, when they are about 6 weeks old and have grown 12 to 15 cm tall, transplant the young plants to their final location, before they are too woody and expanded. The early varieties should be ready around May, the intermediate ones between May and June. Discard all plants that appear weak or free of buds.

The plants must be fixed well, with the first leaf at ground level. The plant distances in principle are around 70 cm between the rows and 50 cm on the row.

Cultivation practices

Just before starting the transplant of young plants from the seedbed, add 90 g of superphosphate mixed with 30 g of potassium sulphate per square meter to the soil.

Hoe regularly to remove weeds and break up the soil surface for aeration. If the weather is dry, wet thoroughly. To reduce watering, which is able to satisfy the high-water requirement of the species, a good mulching could be useful.

About a month after sowing, tuck the soil around the plants to protect them from the winds and put supports on the larger and more exposed ones. Remove the lower leaves when they turn yellow.

Where the sun beats down a lot it can be useful to use shading nets to avoid excessive heat making the sprouts plant suffer.

Cultivation techniques

Rotation: Brussels sprouts must not return to their own soil or to the soil of other cabbages for at least two years, they follow very well legumes (such as peas, broad beans or beans) that enrich the soil with nitrogen.

Association: there are some vegetables that are friendly to sprouts because their presence drives away the cabbage fly; these are tomatoes, celery, rosemary and sage, which are an excellent association.

How to grow Brussels sprouts: harvesting and storage

The early varieties begin to produce in late August or early September, the intermediate varieties have their maximum production in November and December and the late varieties in February and, sometimes, March.

Brussels sprouts must be picked when they have reached the right size and the buds have not yet hatched. Collect a few at a time, working from the bottom up. When starting the harvest, cut off the upper part of the plant, which looks like a cabbage and can be used in soups.

Diseases and parasites

Among the fungal diseases we mention Alternariosis, the cruciferous hernia, the basal rot and the downy mildew.

They are also sensitive to some bacteria (Xanthomonas campestris, Erwinia carotovora).

The most important animal parasites are aphids, nocturnes, cavolaie, elateridae, altica, weevils and the cabbage fly.

Downy mildew can be hindered by spraying horsetail decoction.

Cruciferous hernia and numerous basal and bacteriosis rots are severely limited by correct rotations (avoid the cultivation of any cruciferous plant for 3-4 years on the same plot), by the distribution of lithotamn on the ground before transplanting and by spraying horsetail decoction.

Bacillus is used to control noctuids.

The altica can be a serious problem especially in the case of compact and dry soils; it can be contained in small family gardens with broom branches and sprinkling the vegetation with lithotamn and bentonite. In case of strong attacks use the pyrethrum.

The control of the cabbage fly is above all preventive and essentially consists of the destruction of vegetation residues, possibly also removing the surrounding patch of earth

How to grow Brussels sprouts on the balcony

In a balcony garden, prefer the dwarf varieties, which will not exceed 70-80 cm in height and their harvest will be proportional to the care you offer them.

In general, this cabbage accepts poor soils and does not require particular fertilization, if not a little nitrogen supply during the growth phase; hyper -fertilizing, on the other hand, will result in early flowering, losing part or all of the harvest.

Even if the varieties you choose for the balcony are smaller, they will still need a pot that is at least 40 cm deep in which only one plant can grow. By choosing the woven fiber bags and filling them with 60 cm of soil, you can make up to three plants live together.

Sow the Brussels sprouts in cellular containers placing 2 seeds per cell. Keep the soil moist trying to ensure temperatures around 25°C for the vegetables. To prevent the sun from drying the soil too much, place the containers in the shade immediately after sowing.

After a week or so, the sprout seedlings will sprout from the ground. Water the soil consistently and, once the seedlings have grown a few centimeters, remove the weakest one in each alveolus. About 30-40 days after sowing, when the seedlings have produced 3 or 4 leaves, proceed with the transplant.

Prepare the pots by placing a layer of expanded clay on the bottom, then fill them with well-packed soil. In the center of the pot, make a hole capable of containing the earthen bread of the seedlings, place the Brussels sprout inside and wet it abundantly to facilitate rooting.

Grow Brussels sprout in partial shade while keeping the soil moist. Constantly check the pots by removing weeds and trying to move the earth when it compacts. To avoid these jobs mulch the soil, for sure you will save a lot of energy. If the plants grow in temperatures of around 25°C, you will start harvesting the sprouts less than 45 days after transplanting.

Collect the Brussels sprouts as they grow along the stem of the plant, starting from the bottom and slowly rising upwards. By removing the ripe sprouts, the plant will be stimulated to produce new ones and speed up the ripening process of those already present on the stem.

Use in cooking and therapeutic properties

In the kitchen they are mainly used for the preparation of first courses or side dishes. They can be boiled in plenty of water and salt and then seasoned with oil and spices. They are also excellent sautéed in a pan. Some also use it to prepare baked lasagna, pies or pastes.

Brussels sprouts are rich in minerals (iron, copper, calcium, potassium, manganese and phosphorus) and also contain proteins and carbohydrates. They help in the prevention of breast, prostate and colon cancer thanks to the numerous antioxidants contained in it (thiocyanates, zeaxanthin, indoles, isothiocyanates and sulforaphane).

They abound in vitamins such as vitamin A (useful for the skin and mucous membranes), vitamin B, vitamin C (to protect the body from infections). Also present is vitamin K (useful for bone health and to limit neuronal damage in cases of Alzheimer's).

They are also useful as detoxifiers and to counteract anemia and prevent ulcer formation. The presence of vitamin B1 and folic acid improves concentration and attention. The fibers contained in them help those suffering from constipation and intestinal irregularity.

The amino acids and antioxidants contained in them also help keep blood vessels clean, lowering cholesterol.

CHAPTER 27
HOW TO GROW STRAWBERRIES

Use seedlings purchased in the nursery, as strawberry reproduction by seed is decidedly complex. The soil that will host your strawberry must be well drained to avoid stagnation of water and fertilized with mature manure before implanting the seedlings.

Subsequently, during vegetation, it will be important to integrate waterings with liquid fertilizer containing phosphorus and potassium. You will have to create grooves at a distance of 60/80 centimeters between them, in which you will bury the plants at a distance of about twenty centimeters. After planting, water abundantly.

The planting of strawberries must take place in the middle of the summer season: this allows the seedlings to grow just enough to face the winter in the best possible way and give the best fruiting in the following spring.

Strawberries need constant and abundant watering, taking care to always and only wet the soil, never the strawberries or the leaves. Although strawberries do not suffer particularly from low temperatures, if you live in an area where winter is particularly harsh it is advisable to protect the seedlings with a layer of mulch made up of leaves and straw or with the special protective sheets that you find in any good garden. center.

An important caveat. Strawberries, if left free to grow without any constraints, tend to expand rapidly. If you particularly love strawberries, this is fine, but if you want to avoid this pest effect, keep them under control and prune them whenever they get out of line.

CHAPTER 28
FILLING A CASSETTE

Before the planning and preparation phase, it is necessary to identify where the box will be placed: whether in the garden in direct contact with the ground or on a balcony or terrace not in direct contact with the ground. The right model and a sunny location are decisive factors.

Autumn and spring are the best times.

To fill the raised box, you can proceed in different ways depending on whether or not the box has a continuous bottom and is or is therefore not in direct contact with the ground. Below we explain both types in detail:

Raised box in direct contact with the ground

It can be filled either with materials found in nature (branches, bushes, kitchen scraps, etc.) or with packaged products from the DIY Garden assortment. If the raised box is made of wood, it is best not to place it directly on the ground, to make it last longer. It is advisable to first dig a hollow of about 20 - 30 cm in the ground with a perimeter about 5 cm larger than the raised box. The hollow is then filled with gravel.

To prevent moles and the like from eating the cultivated vegetables, before filling, insert a mouse protection net on the bottom. To effectively protect the internal wooden walls from wet, apply a drainage membrane.

How should I proceed to properly fill the raised box?

It is essential to create an appropriate drainage layer to have a fertile garden. We recommend the use of light and stable expanded clay, which, depending on the height of the garden, constitutes ¼ or at most ⅓ of the height of the cultivation bed. Applying a separating fiber on top of the expanded clay prevents soil from entering the drainage layer during watering. A layer of garden compost or composted earth generates decomposition heat as a result of organic stratification and serves as a growth engine for vegetables.

To this must be added a layer of universal soil or soil for vegetables that can be completed with a little soil for sowing and aromatic herbs. Adding a weekly organic universal fertilizer to the water used for watering helps your vegetables grow quickly and provides all the nutrients needed for a growing season. In vegetable gardens set up on a balcony, the earth is depleted faster and is replaced at least partially once a year.

CHAPTER 29
THE "LASAGNA" VEGETABLE GARDEN

Begun in the United States around the nineties, the "lasagna" garden is composed of several layers of different and superimposed materials, exactly like a Bolognese lasagna, hence the name. The procedure with the garden in which it is made is very important. It is advisable to respect the sequence in which the materials are arranged, in order to avoid creating a simple inert heap on which nothing will grow.

The "lasagna" garden adopts the "do-nothing" idea of Masanobu Fukuoka, a method that consists of refraining from any weeding, fertilizing and pruning, simply letting nature take its course.

The "lasagna" vegetable garden is a possible solution in the case of poor or polluted soils. Being raised off the ground makes work more accessible and less tiring.

The advantages are many: fewer weeds, better water retention, due to the fact that the compost retains water, especially if the native soil is sandy. Always, compost allows you to reduce the amount of fertilizer, as it releases the nutrients little by little. The soil is then easier to work because it is crumbly, loose and soft.

Materials to make it:

- recovered paper / cardboard
- biological material source of nitrogen
- biological material that is a source of carbon
- compost
- mulch material, such as dry leaves, pine needles, straw

Construction method:

1) Cartons

After identifying the dedicated area and delimiting it with a wooden frame that can be obtained by recycling boards or pallets, the cartons are placed on the ground, very close (without printing or stickers), taking care to make them overlap. They should then be moistened with water. The cardboard will serve as an "anti-weed" barrier.

2) Green waste

Continue with a layer of green waste, such as fruit or vegetable peels, vegetable waste or cut grass. Basically all the vegetable waste that usually find their places in the compost.

3) Brown waste

The third layer is made up of materials usually found in brown compost such as straw, hay, dead leaves, pine needles, mowing scraps, peat.

4) Mature compost

The formation of the lasagna garden continues with a mature compost layer or a mixture made up half soil and half compost.

It is advisable to wait a week or two before planting. It is in fact necessary to ensure that the temperature in the center of the lasagna garden, derived from the fermentation of vegetable residues, is not too high because the heat could compromise the germination capacity of the seeds.

In terms of quantity and sequence of brown and green waste layers, Jean Paul Collaert, a specialist in this method, favors layers up to 10-15 cm thick (cardboard, green, brown, green, brown, mature compost ....).

The advantages of cultivating with the "lasagna" garden

Simple maintenance: the raised garden facilitates planting and care of vegetables.

Savings: irrigation is reduced thanks to the use of mulch which is spread between the vegetables thus keeping the soil moist.

Recycling of all the organic elements available (eg kitchen organic, pruning waste, leaves, grass clippings, cartons, etc.).

Fertilizer, compost, mulch can be distributed in a targeted way and without waste.

Reduction of weeds always thanks to mulching and denser planting of vegetables.

Productivity increase derived from denser planting of vegetables.

More variety of plants, thanks to the soil conditions that can be varied in each bed creating the possibility of growing plants that like different soil characteristics such as acid soil, greater drainage, specific orientation...

Better drainage because the soil around the plants is not trampled, ideal in the case of clayey soils.

Improved cultivation times, for example, the cultivation period can be extended because raised beds tend to heat up earlier in the spring and remain productive longer.

Fewer pest problems. The creation of biodiversity involves fewer attacks by parasites on vegetables thanks to the planting in synergy of garden-friendly plants, such as pest repellers, plants capable of attracting useful, aromatic insects, flowers.

Versatility: the vegetable garden can become a very beautiful aesthetic element, useful for exploiting productivity in more limited spaces even at home and if well done, even disabled people can take care of it.

CHAPTER 30
THE SOIL

The earth is a living thing and it is up to us to keep it so when, in its management, we replace mother nature.

FIELD SOIL

Field soil is what you find in house gardens, if you have it, or in cultivated fields, in woods, in meadows, in construction sites where excavations are carried out.

You can also buy it at a good price in some nurseries. On average it is 90% inorganic and 10% organic. The exact composition is decided by nature for uncultivated land. In addition to this solid component, in the soil there is a conspicuous gaseous component consisting of the air that circulates in free spaces, essential for the breathing of the roots that develop. From this we understand how important it is to keep the soil airy and oxygenated.

HEAVY OR CLAY SOIL

Clay. The inorganic part is made up of very fine particles, with a diameter of less than 2 microns. To understand if a ground is clayey, just wet it a little and squeeze it in one hand: if it is easily modeled it is clay. It also sticks to shoes, hands and tools. When it is dry it is crumbly and dusty. Clayey soil has the defect of being not very permeable to water and air. If clay is present in excessive quantities, it tends to cause water stagnation which can cause the roots to rot. If, on the other hand, the altitude is moderate, it has the advantage of retaining water and nutrients. A clayey soil is corrected by adding river sand, which favors water drainage and air circulation, and humus-rich soil that lightens its structure and enhances its fertility.

LIGHT OR SANDY SOIL

The inorganic part is made up of larger particles, with a diameter between 50 microns and 2 millimeters. Sandy soil can be recognized because squeezing a wet handful of it does not compact but crumbles. It has the defect of letting itself be permeated too easily by the water, which flows through it without being absorbed in adequate quantities by the roots. Pure nutrients are soon washed away with a consequent reduction in fertility. In addition, it heats up very easily even at depth, increasing the need for water. If the sand is not excessive, it has the advantage of favoring water drainage and air circulation, avoiding the danger of rot and asphyxiation of the soil. Sandy soil is corrected by adding loamy soil and fertile loam.

SILTY SOIL

The famous one left by the floods of the Nile. The inorganic part is mainly made up of particles between 2 and 75 microns. It is a cross between sandy and clayey soil, with the strengths and weaknesses of both. If present in a high proportion, silt poses fertility problems, and with the rain it forms a very hard crust.

SOIL OF MEDIUM-TEXTURE

Is the best. With clay, sand and silt present in the right proportions.

PH

Yes, the pH must also be taken into account. Soils are divided into acidic, neutral, basic and alkaline. The ideal soil for growing vegetables has a pH tending to neutral. Universal soils are usually slightly acidic. The packets will indicate the vegetables with particular pH requirements. For those who need acidic soil it is sufficient to increase the amount of soil or add peat or organic fertilizers to the potting mix. To obtain an alkaline soil, you can add elemental sulfur (it is allowed in organic farming), available in garden centers, or even some wood ash burned in the fireplace.

TOPSOIL

There are two types. There is the natural one that covers the surface of wooded soils, soft and rich in organic plant residues (leaves, degraded shrubs, etc.) and animals (manure and remains). Mole soil is also natural, formed by the excavation of moles and accumulated in those mounds with a hole in the center that is not difficult to see when walking around woods and meadows. And then there is industrial soil, prepared by man, bagged and sold in garden centers. This soil also consists of an organic and an inorganic part. In the industrial sector, the organic component usually consists of peat and / or compost derived from the composting of the organic fraction of solid urban waste. There should always be a good amount of humus, a precious nutrient produced by earthworms starting from organic substances.

The inorganic component is made up of various types of inert materials which give structure and guarantee water drainage as well as porosity: sand, clay, pumice, volcanic lapillus, perlite. The soils are of various types, but the universal one is fine for your home garden as long as it is of good quality, generally indicated by the higher price, as well as by the label. It is sold in packs of 5 to 80 liters. Don't be frightened by the weight: a liter of soil weighs less than 300 grams, so a 20-liter pack weighs around 6 kilos, a transportable burden. If you can count on a pair of strong arms, yours or those of available people, do not hesitate to choose a maxi pack because it is cheaper.

TO IMPROVE THE GROUND

PEAT

An organic fossil substance extracted from natural deposits, peat bogs, it represents the first stage in the process of transforming plants into coal. It also contains remains of animals and insects that give it nourishing properties, so it also acts as a fertilizer. It has an acidic pH and retains water so keeps the soil moist. There is blond peat (sphagnum or moss), less decomposed, more acidic and with a low quantity of nutrients, and dark peat, more decomposed, less acidic and richer in humus and mineral salts. To counter the danger of peatland depletion, some soil producers replace peat with more environmentally sustainable coconut fiber.

COCONUT

Unlike peat it has a neutral pH. It increases the ability of the soil to retain water and promotes aeration. It is sold in very light and easy-to-carry tiles.

SILICA SAND (OR RIVER SAND)

The sand that is often spoken of in horticulture is not that of the sea but that of rivers. Sand increases the draining capacity of a soil by preventing water stagnation and its penetration, which is essential in the cultivation of carrots. You can find it on the banks of rivers if one flows near your home, or in hardware centers (often of French origin) that, in addition to DIY, deal with building materials and gardening items. It is sold in bags of 20-30 kilos at the more than affordable price of around 10 cents per kilo.

CHAPTER 31
CREATE A SELF-SUFFICIENT GARDEN

A vegetable garden is a fun and satisfying spring-summer activity. The concept of self-sufficiency is really important right now, as environmental sustainability is becoming a necessity rather than a choice.

There are many reasons that lead to the creation of a vegetable garden at home: passion for nature, the desire to have products personally controlled, a pleasant hobby and anti-stress.

These days, reflecting on the "return to nature" trend leads us to think about how advantageous it is to live in a house with a vegetable garden. Whether it is large or small, the self-production of fruit and vegetables guarantees us the possibility of eating healthier products, richer in vitamins and minerals, but above all not to worry about how to get food to put on the table.

Permaculture

Design a vegetable garden to grow the vegetables your family prefers, then find the best corner of your yard (or patio) to plant them. With a little time and care, your patch of land will be filled with delicious produce. We talk about permaculture: it is a cultivation method that, on the basis of ecological principles and strategies, allows us to design agricultural settlements similar to natural ecosystems, and therefore able to maintain themselves independently and renew themselves with low use of energy.

Most people interested in permaculture work in domestic contexts - a detached house or an apartment with a small garden. Permaculture works great in small spaces and is ideal in this kind of situation. Let's see together some cultivation methods typical of permaculture to make your vegetable garden or garden healthy, in need of little work and above all very productive.

Soil is the basis of life on our planet. The food web of the soil is complex and delicate, and perhaps the worst thing we can do to it is regularly turn and break the earth. Traditionally we dig to loosen it and create soil suitable for sowing, incorporating fertilizers and removing weeds. There are so many ways to avoid digging regularly, so that we not only save the soil, but also a lot of energy.

Raised bed cultivation, also called caissons, is a super easy way to grow without digging. The cultivation area is divided into permanent boxes of the size suitable for the grower. Make sure that the center can be easily reached from any direction around it. Boxes do not necessarily have rigid materials around the edges, although some prefer to make them to keep grass out, grow vegetables beyond the reach of rabbits and whiteflies, or to make it easier for even those with limited movement to reach them.

The soil on the surface of the caissons is deep, rich and can support a high density of plants, which therefore can be cultivated at a short distance from each other, less than that usually observed. Compost is added to the bins every year and, as in nature, soil life incorporates it by taking it from the surface and bringing it down to convert it into nutrients.

Polyculture is the opposite of monoculture, it means growing more than one type of plant in the same space. It can be as simple as growing salad in the spaces between cabbages, or as complex as a two-acre forest garden. An example of a monoculture is a wheat field or a plot of only broccoli. When root bacteria encounter an entire brassica area they have free range and multiply, causing very serious damage. Pests and diseases tend to specialize in a particular species, which is why they look for a specific plant. This is why traditional wants us to rotate crop species in different areas, to avoid the proliferation of these pathogens.

Polyculture mimics nature and makes it harder for pathogens to find their favorite plants, as well as the fact that when they find one, they don't find them all.

By observing nature, we can see how plants live together while being different in both shape and size; for light, water and nutrient needs; by growth rate and harvesting periods. Diversity makes optimal use of available resources; every niche is filled with life.

With their differences, plants can create beneficial conditions for each other, such as salads under broccoli for example - salads will benefit from light shade in the summer months. By filling the boxes with vegetables we have to weed less and we have more food. Let's not forget, however, that we always have to replace what we collect and this intensive growth requires new compost for the bins every season.

Mulching simply consists of covering the soil with non-living matter. The soil never wants to be bare in nature: it is usually covered with a carpet of leaves, vegetation, material from dead plants, nutrients of animal origin, etc.

For growers, mulching serves various functions, depending on what it is made of and when a weed barrier is applied to:

Kill or suppress them and to prevent others from germinating,

Prevent soil erosion due to wind and rain,

Reduce the evaporation of water due to the sun.

The vegetables to be planted must be studied carefully: consider whether they require a cold wave to start, or if they will wilt and then die when the temperatures drop. If you live in a climate that has very short summers or in an area with scarcity of water, for example, you will need to pay special attention to your choice of plants.

Remove the weeds: as the vegetables sprout, you may notice seedlings that take advantage of fertilization and irrigation. Pick up the weed near the roots and pull gently, then throw it away so the weeds don't take root. Be careful not to remove the newly hatched vegetables.

CHAPTER 32
HOW TO GROW ZUCCHINI

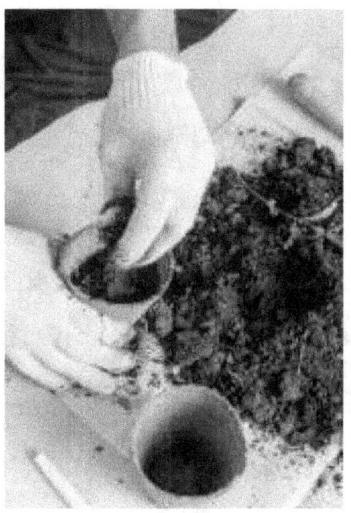

How to grow zucchini in pots on the balcony. They are harvested from May to September.

Zucchini are rich in water, fiber, vitamins, mineral salts.

They are in fact a perfect ingredient for the preparation of many delicious recipes, from appetizers to desserts, courgettes are a vegetable really rich in properties that are important for our health as well as for our physical shape, since they contain a high amount of water.

THE NUTRITIONAL PROPERTIES OF ZUCCHINI

They contain mineral salts, especially potassium, iron, phosphorus and vitamins, especially E and those of group B. But not only that: courgettes are also a source of lutein, an important carotenoid for eye health. Not to mention that the peel is rich in carotenoids and folic acid. There are therefore many good reasons not only to bring courgettes to the table often but also to grow them in pots directly on the balcony or terrace.

HOW TO GROW ZUCCHINI

The cultivation of zucchini does not take long: just place the plant in a fairly sunny area and water it regularly. Here's how to proceed:

First of all, choose the round zucchini, more suitable for growing in pots or the climbing varieties to grow on special supports.

The right time to proceed with the sowing of zucchini in pots is from April to the beginning of May. The sowing in the seedbed must take place instead around February-March: in this case, as soon as the sprouts have put on some leaves and reached 8-12 centimeters in height, you must transfer them to a pot at least 40-45 centimeters wide. If, on the other hand, you have more space available in the garden, take advantage of it and space the plants apart by at least 80 cm, preferably one meter.

The soil must be very fertile for the fruit to develop. It is estimated that 30-40 kg of manure or compost must be added for 10 square meters of soil. In pots, it is necessary to use spacious and deep containers since the root of the plant tends to go deep.

To ensure that the soil is always well drained and to avoid water stagnation, cover the bottom of the pot with gravel or expanded clay.

Also choose good soil and bury the plants or seeds using a wooden awl.

After transplanting the seedling, cover with a light layer of mulch. To avoid the growth of weeds it would be good to mulch the soil either with straw or with special sheets.

If you decide to grow climbing zucchini, also provide yourself with sticks with which to support the plants and threads with which to tie them in order to support them well.

Make sure that the plant has plenty of light.

Remember to water the seedlings often, even twice a day if necessary, especially in the early morning and in the evening at sunset.

As for the harvest, it generally takes place from May to September depending on the period of sowing and the area in which it is carried out and in addition to the courgettes it will also allow you to collect courgette flowers. There are early and late varieties that can bear fruit until late autumn.

Also remember not to put the courgettes in the same area for two years in a row.

CHAPTER 33
GROWING AROMATIC PLANTS AT HOME

In order not to give up the flavors of Mediterranean cuisine even in winter, the secret is to grow aromatic herbs on the terrace, protected by a warm box. Here's how it's done.

Growing aromatic annuals on the terrace is possible. For the more rustic and resistant species, such as rosemary and laurel, protection from the cold is sufficient by moving the pot into a sheltered position (for example, leaning it against a wall) or covering it with a non-woven fabric, light and breathable. Other aromatic species on the terrace are more sensitive to low temperatures, for example basil, mint, tarragon, lemon balm and sage, and can only be grown in pots outdoors if properly placed in a balcony greenhouse or in a warm bed box.

Prepare the structure for the aromatic herbs

The hot bed box is prepared in this way.

Prepare a large empty planter (approximate dimensions 100 x 40 cm), preferably in concrete or terracotta, with a removable glass cover.

Inside put a first basal layer of expanded clay (2 cm), then an intermediate layer of manure (10 cm) and, in the highest part, a layer (15-20 cm) of universal soil mixed with peat.

The aromatic plants, purchased in pots, must be extracted from the jar and, once the roots have been untangled, transplanted into the box. Then the seedlings should be wet well. Finally, cover the caisson with the glass plate.

How the caisson works

The use of manure, of bovine or equine origin, is necessary because the fermentation of this fresh material generates heat and the structure of the box, closed at the top, ensures that the heat produced is retained inside, maintaining the necessary temperature for these seedlings to live even in winter. Unfortunately, fresh manure is a difficult material to find; it can be found at a farm or at an equestrian center.

Three treatments can suffice.

The care required for the cultivation of herbs on the terrace placed in the hot bed box are few.

1. Water the seedlings as soon as they are planted. Subsequently, water them only when necessary, if the soil dries out, without exaggerating.

2. During the coldest days and in the evening, it is advisable to cover the glass of the herbs with straw (you can buy it in a garden center, in various sizes and dimensions), in order to increase the insulation and maintain the temperature even during the night.

3. On sunny days, on the other hand, during the central hours of the day, open the glass to air the aromatic herbs on the terrace.

CHAPTER 34
HOW TO GROW CARROTS

Carrots are a very common horticultural plant. The edible part of the plant is the long and thick tap root, it contains many nutrients and is excellent for the preparation of many dishes such as soups, fresh side dishes, rice salads, sauces and fillings.

The optimal growth and development of carrots occur in conditions of stable temperature. Sudden changes in temperature can in fact slow down if not completely stop their growth. Carrots therefore prefer constant temperatures of around 18-20 degrees and average humidity, they absolutely do not tolerate too humid or stagnant soils.

Prepare the ground

Carrots, to grow at their best, therefore must receive special care. A very important point that determines the success of this crop is the soil, so let's see its characteristics in detail.

The sowing of carrots is carried out in loose soil, this is a fundamental requirement. In fact the root (which is the edible part) must be able to develop freely without encountering obstacles such as stones or other large objects. Furthermore, clayey soils, being too compact, can hinder their development as well as prevent the normal flow of water, causing dangerous stagnation.

The planting of carrots requires a medium-textured soil, loose, rich in organic substance and with a good percentage of sand that allows the flow of water. Calcareous soils with a pH between 6.5 and 7.5 are indicated.

The soil must be prepared in the summer, a deep hoeing is carried out and at the same time, if necessary, organic fertilizer or well decomposed manure is incorporated into the soil.

How to sow

Once you have worked the ground you can proceed with sowing. Planting carrots is possible all year round, in the open field, however, you have to consider the minimum temperatures and possibly choose to grow them indoors in greenhouses or boxes and then transplant them to your garden as soon as the weather permits.

The early sowing is carried out in boxes or greenhouses in the period from October to February, the plants grown in this way will produce the first harvest after about 90-100 days.

Further south, cultivation can start as early as February-March, in this case short-length varieties will be chosen which are more suitable for the type of early cultivation.

In the period of spring and summer it is possible to carry out further sowing, with varieties suitable for the period. Sowing done in August will need winter protection, which is done with straw or similar material to ensure a slightly higher temperature.

There are different methods to cultivate carrots, but the most used ones are broadcaster sowing and row sowing. Broadcast sowing is generally used for small flower beds where, due to the reduced space, it is more convenient than row sowing.

Broadcasting, given the small size of the seed, is often carried out by mixing fine sand with the seeds, in this way a more uniform distribution will be obtained and seed accumulations will be avoided. After distributing the seeds, it is advisable to obtain thin soil to be distributed evenly on the flower bed, after which a light watering can be carried out.

The cultivation of carrots in rows involves the preparation of small grooves spaced 20cm apart, the seeds will be placed in number of 1-3, spacing them about 7cm from each other.

The germination of the seedlings takes place in about 15-20 days, in this period and until the plants have reached at least a height of 15-20cm, constant control on weeds must be carried out also because the growth is quite slow and the seedlings could be easily suffocated.

If broadcast sowing has been chosen, the thinning of the seedlings will be a must, the sowing between the rows still requires control and you will have to leave a plant every 7cm approximately.

Thinning is done when the seedlings have shown the second or third leaf; avoid thinning the crop when the soil is dry, it is always a good idea to do it when the soil is damp and soft, the seedlings will come off much more easily and you will avoid damage the remaining ones.

Another very important aspect of carrot cultivation is the humidity of the soil, we have said that there must not be water stagnation, but too dry soil is not good either. For summer crops grown in areas where there is little rainfall, a water supply is required which varies according to the type of soil and the duration of the drought. In any case, during the first stages of plant development it is necessary to carry out constant and continuous watering.

How they are harvested

Carrot harvesting is usually done after about 90-100 days from sowing. Some varieties have different ripening periods that you need to know before sowing.

For harvesting it is advisable that the soil is moderately humid, this facilitates uprooting and minimizes any damage. Carrots are harvested by grabbing the aerial part evenly and gently pulling the root from the ground without tugging.

How are they preserved?

After harvesting, the carrots must be cleaned of any traces of earth and placed in layers in a dry and cool place. They can be kept in the fridge in the fruit section for a few months.

Fertilization

Providing carrot plants with a good supply of manure or organic compost can ensure optimal growth and a good harvest. Generally, 3-4 kg of mature manure are administered per square meter of cultivation when the soil is prepared. It is important that the fertilizer is well decomposed as fermentation can lead to root rot.

CHAPTER 35
FINAL TIPS

Who knows why, but the vegetables grown in our garden, even if not exactly aesthetically perfect, have a different flavor, they seem more appetizing, perhaps because they are seasoned with the effort of producing them!

Creating raised flower beds in a garden or making boxes with a refined appearance satisfies the lovers of an elegant and tidy garden, and is an excellent way to exploit otherwise unusable small areas.

Raised beds are well known and widespread in the Anglo-Saxon world, they are the so-called "garden boxes".

They can be made by yourself, perhaps by recycling objects, or on the market there are boxes or tubs of various sizes ready for use.

All vegetables, especially small ones, benefit most from cultivation in raised ground.

The benefits are varied and, thanks to these factors, productivity is significantly increased, irrigation management, weed control and fertilization are easier to conduct.

The first to benefit from an elevated garden is our back, as it does not need to bend down for periodic maintenance.

Even a disabled person can operate one while sitting comfortably in the wheelchair.

The creation of a vegetable garden inside caissons can be a nice idea to bring children closer to the pleasure and knowledge of nature, a way to have fun being together while admiring a world "within reach".

SOIL

The boxes can be filled with any type of soil desired without having to adapt the botanical choices of the vegetables to the characteristics of the original soil of the place, the soil inside a container can be replaced as desired, whenever desired.

IRRIGATION

Less compact soil ensures better drainage, the sides of the

caissons maintain higher humidity and retain mulch and fertilizers.

I recommend a drip irrigation system that guarantees the right amount of water with consequent water savings.

TEMPERATURE AND LIGHT

A crop placed on a higher level than the floor receives more light, a very useful factor especially in the seasons when light is scarce.

The soil contained inside the box heats up more easily, and planting, germination and growth of the seedlings will be early.

Attention! Verifying the hydration of the raised garden will be an important factor so check the soil frequently.

SPACES

The tubs can be made in the desired shape and size by exploiting the available spaces and following a harmonious design adaptable to the style of the garden or terrace that will contain them.

The spaces inside the beds can be divided in a targeted and organized way in order to increase productivity, in a raised bed the plants can be positioned closer to each other for the greatest available light.

FIGHT AGAINST UNWANTED INSECTS

In such confined spaces it is easy to apply a protective net that keeps harmful insects and snails away and helps to protect the produce from heavy rain and wind.

Aromatic herbs and flowers are ideal companions for vegetables in a raised garden, providing scents and colors to brighten up the spaces.

Raised bed crops have gained popularity over the past decade or so. These raised beds, or "vegetable boxes", serve as a decorative element, and also offer numerous benefits to the gardener, such as making cultivation less strenuous, simplifying the management of weeds and pests, lengthening the growing season and, potentially, increasing the yield of the crop.

If you are thinking of making a raised vegetable garden, or have already built one, do not miss these precious tricks to optimize cultivation!

1. Use lightweight construction materials

As you begin planning your raised garden, it's important to carefully consider the materials. If possible, avoid heavy woods, track beams and concrete blocks. Choose thin wood panels, which are lighter. The caissons will still be quite heavy, but easier to move in case of need.

2. Do not exceed 120 cm in width

The main idea of a raised garden is to create a cultivable space that is easily accessible and contains high quality soil. This means creating a flower bed on a human scale.

3. Cover the bottom with cardboard

Weeds are a common nuisance to all farmable spaces. Spread a layer of thick cardboard on the ground (or cut grass) at the base of the bin, making sure to cover it all. This solution will prevent germinating weed seeds from making their way to the surface.

4. Add a layer of cut grass or dead leaves

The most expensive aspect of building a raised garden is filling it with potting soil. To cut costs a little, you can sprinkle a thick layer of partially decomposed cut grass or dead leaves on the bottom before filling with soil. In addition to saving you some money, these organic materials will decompose over time, enriching the soil with nutrients.

5. Insert pipes to hold the cover sheets

The covers for the rows and the nets for birds are essential accessories for the crops. They shelter plants from strong sun and extreme temperatures, as well as keep birds and insects away. Before filling with earth, secure vertical segments of PVC pipes along the internal walls of the caisson. When it comes time to cover the plants, tuck the ends of the sheet support structures into these tubes.

6. Autumn mulch

During the fall, remove any plant residue from the raised bed and sprinkle the bare earth with a layer of mulch of about 5-8 cm. Mulch will preserve soil moisture during the winter, as well as release nutrients as it decomposes.

From ancient origins, the raised garden has returned in great vogue in recent years because it allows you to grow vegetables even in the city. The raised garden is an excellent solution for those who do not want to give up growing vegetables, benefiting from the many advantages it brings. First of all, the raised vegetable garden performs a protective function for the plants it contains, both in summer, offering shelter from parasites, and in the colder months, protecting them from the cold and ensuring better exposure to sunlight. Secondly, it even allows to double the productivity of the cultivated products, thanks to three fundamental elements:

The soil: much more fertile than the classic home garden as it is more porous (it is not trampled on).

The light: it seems strange but in the raised garden the plants receive more light, despite being a few centimeters from the ground. This allows plants to benefit from the sun's rays in greater quantities, especially in winter, when the sunlight is dimmer.

The temperature: again by virtue of its location higher than the ground, the soil of the raised garden heats up faster, so as to facilitate both germination and growth.

Other advantages can be: the convenience of not having to bend over too much, the ease of crop rotation, but also the more accurate control of weeds and pathogens and the practicality inherent in the raised vegetable garden: you can easily reach the center of the box.

The practicality of the wooden box

In the beginning, the containment walls of raised gardens were made of woven wood, in particular that of willow. Subsequently we moved on to the use of wooden boxes, much more practical and solid. Within these forms we can arrange the plants as we wish, even if it is more convenient to adopt a specific criterion, such as arranging the plants in groups of three.

Only if it is truly stainless does metal offer first-rate aesthetic and functional solutions: first of all, by choosing a box made of stainless steel, you can create a raised garden that has an extremely thin perimeter wall, provided that it is not very long. The excessive length of the sides of the caisson in fact, could cause loosening and deformity phenomena that can compromise the stability of our raised garden. If the metal is welded and not bent, you need to be sure that the weld is done well and that it does not fail. Finally, don't forget to make at least one drain hole in the caisson.

There are plants that need to develop vertically: for example cherry tomatoes, beans, green beans and peas, which otherwise would end up intertwining and suffocating each other, obviously to the detriment of production.

You can build trellises of willow or bamboo canes, around which to pass some raffia to ensure that the plants adhere better.

For the terrace in the city

We have said several times that the revival of the raised garden coincided with the trends towards recycling, healthy living and attention to nature that has erupted in recent years. It is therefore not difficult to find a terrace or a large balcony with a garden flanked by a raised vegetable garden in the city center, since for many the do-it-yourself cultivation of vegetables and fruit has become a necessity.

Industrial pallets can help in this type of solution: these wooden pallets are very useful in terms of solidity and are very long lasting, even if subjected to bad weather and daily watering.

The pallets can be placed in any direction, flat, vertically, tilted, cut, disassembled and reassembled as needed.

www.ingramcontent.com/pod-product-compliance
Lightning Source LLC
Chambersburg PA
CBHW072055110526
44590CB00018B/3179